Wholehearted Integration

Wholehearted Integration

Harmonizing Psychology and Christianity Through Word and Deed

Kirk E. Farnsworth

BAKER BOOK HOUSE
Grand Rapids, Michigan 49506

ISBN: 0-8010-3515-9

Library of Congress
Catalog Card Number: 85-071175

Printed in the United States of America

Contents

Acknowledgments

This book has emerged from a combination of interactions in a variety of contexts. Consequently, I am indebted to many persons who have over the past several years had a hand in the formation of my ideas. First are the students in the integration seminars that I have taught at Wheaton College and Trinity College, who have stimulated me with their spirited interaction and intellectual curiosity. Second, my own mentors in the graduate program at Iowa State University, my colleagues at the University of New Hampshire, and the psychology faculty at Duquesne University, who have given me a thorough understanding of and appreciation for psychology as both a natural science and a human science. In addition, I appreciate the faculty of Fuller Theological Seminary, who turned me on during a postdoctoral fellowship to the excitement of theological research, and the faculty of the Department of Biblical, Theological and Archaeological Studies at Wheaton College, who recently invited me to conduct a series of faculty development seminars on psychological factors in biblical interpretation.

I have also benefited greatly from interaction with associates in various disciplines who participated in my integration seminars during the annual Trinity College Faith/Learning/Living Institute. Equally beneficial has been the forum given me by the *Journal of Psychology and Theology* for professional interaction on my ideas regarding the conduct of integration and the integration issues of rationalism and professionalism. And, by graciously providing the resources for me to initiate an annual conference for Christian college psychology professors, the Christian College Coalition has given us an ongoing opportunity to discuss a wide range of integration issues that relate to the teaching of psychology.

Among the many individuals along the road to publishing this book, there are several who stand out. Al Dueck and Michael De Vries have inspired me as exemplars of critical integrative thinking. Rich Butman has been very supportive through our team-taught integration seminars and, along with John Lee, has been a significant help in organizing the aforementioned integration conferences for Christian college psychology professors. For facilitating the actual writing of the book, I would like to thank Ward Kriegbaum, Vice President for Academic Affairs at Wheaton College, for a very generous faculty development writing grant. I would also like to thank Allan Fisher, Textbook Editor for Baker Book House, for his faith in this project from its very beginning and his constant encouragement in seeing it through to publication, and Steve Evans for reading the entire manuscript and sharing his helpful insights. And I am especially grateful for Gerrie Carlson's diligence and excellence in typing the manuscript.

Last but certainly not least, I want to thank my family—Rosie, Craig, Eric, and Kristi—for their patience and understanding when my preoccupation with writing made me a little "spacey." Also, I want to acknowledge the support and encouragement I have received from my church, Calvary Community Church. And finally, I would like to acknowledge the One with whom walking is integrating. To Him be the glory.

Introduction

"Can someone be crazy and still be a Christian?" Or as one recent best seller put it, Why do bad things happen to good people? And when they do, I am often asked, "Should a Christian go to a non-Christian therapist?"

I have also been challenged by more than one university student, "Doesn't science disprove the Bible?" And at the other extreme is the inevitable question from the wide-eyed evangelical Christian student, "What do you think about demon possession?"

These are some of the questions being asked today by people who are interested in both the psychological and the religious aspects of life. Some are just curious, while others would like to harmonize the two in some meaningful way. I share their curiosity as harmonizing as the inclination for unity. In fact, I have been working at uniting psychology and Christianity for many years.

Others have been working as well, in a variety of ways. One of the most interesting attempts at bringing psychology and religion together in the history of this country has been the mind-cure movement. Beginning in the Civil War era and continuing to this day, countless practitioners have been involved, some of the most famous being Mary Baker Eddy, Norman Vincent Peale, and Oral Roberts. Historian Donald Meyer's book, *The Positive Thinkers,* is a brilliant analysis of the entire movement.[1]

According to Meyer, mind cure was compromised from the start. Although it has been very much a part of the changes in American culture through the years, mind cure has usually been little more than religion as pop psychology. In some cases it has been nothing less than pseudotheology in the guise of pseudo-psychology. Norman Vincent Peale, for example, propped up his entire approach with the following assumption, quoted from his book, *You Can Win*: "God will do anything for you that down in your heart you really want him to do. . . . He will actually give you strength, peace, happiness, and boundless well-being if . . . you sincerely want these advantages and desire them enough to take them."[2]

Many of the more recent books that consciously attempt to relate psychology and religion, however, reflect a higher quality of psychology than those in the past. This is probably because more professional psychologists are getting into the act. A noteworthy example is *Healing Love,* coauthored by the prominent psychologist Everett Shostrom.[3] Another example is *Inflation, Poortalk, and the Gospel,* a book that is unique in illustrating how modern experimental psychology and the Christian religion can be interrelated and applied.[4] The following is representative of the authors' approach:

> There is a psychological as well as a theological reason why obedience and faith go together: Our behavior shapes our attitudes. . . . This is one of the most interesting and extensively documented discoveries of recent social-psychological research. . . . Jesus knew this principle and applied it to our economic life when he said, "For where your treasure is, there will your heart be also" (Matthew 6:21). . . . Jesus is suggesting that we can . . . change our heart's attachments by redirecting our investments from financial security to the work of his kingdom.[5]

There are many, many more volumes depicting the products of relating psychology and Christianity that I could cite. It will be more fruitful, however, to discuss the actual process of relating the two. What is the nature of the process for harmonizing psychology and Christianity? But first, what shall we call the process? Let us give it a name.

The Name of the Game

Several terms for relating psychological and religious realities have been suggested. Well-known psychologist Jerome Frank, a self-proclaimed agnostic, suggests that reconciling scientific and more mystical realities should be referred to as a process of *translation*.[6] Some Christian psychologists have also used this term.[7] Their intent has been to show that the same thing can be said in many different ways or languages.

Secular psychologist Sigmund Koch argues that when two different language systems are brought together, the process should be called *cumulation*.[8] In other words, when we go from one language to the other we change our perspective, and perspectives do not fuse but rather multiply. Christian psychologist J. Harold Ellens agrees with the emphasis on perspective.[9] He insists that psychology and theology must not be fused together so that one absorbs the other, but rather theology must be done from a psychological perspective and psychology must be done from a theological perspective.

Some Christian psychologists have suggested the terms *interface*[10] and *synthesis*[11] to represent the reciprocal interaction of psychological and theological perspectives. *Integration,* however, is the term that is most consistently used in the literature. It is the term I will use to refer to the uniting, but not the fusing, of psychology and theology. Integration is the process whereby both disciplines retain their own identity while benefiting from each other's perspective and communicating the same truth.

The Nature of the Beast

Integration actually involves more than the reciprocal interaction of perspectives. Thinking Christianly about psychology and psychologically about Christianity is not all there is to it. This becomes readily apparent when we begin to look at the nature of the integration process. Suddenly we discover that several important issues complicate the integration task and that true unity of two interacting perspectives can only be accomplished by moving beyond thinking integrative thoughts to living them out in our daily walk.

Any thoughts we have that we intend to integrate are affected first and foremost by the methodological issue. Methodology is the starting point of integration, because we want our thoughts to be valid thoughts. We could integrate erroneous thoughts, but it would not make much sense to do so. Thoughts are as valid or erroneous as the process by which we arrive at them. If, for example, we want to integrate what we know from the Bible and what we know about people, our theology and our psychology had better be sound.

Christian psychologist Gary Collins has suggested that psychology would be more sound if it were built on a theistic foundation.[12] Perhaps it would be even more sound if it were theistic throughout its entire structure. What if the presuppositions, methodology, and applications of findings were all given a theistic flavor? We would have a truly transformed psychology. The question is *Would a transformed psychology enhance the quality of integration?* That is the psychological form of the methodological issue that will be discussed further in chapter 1.

There is also a theological form of the methodological issue. This is because theological methods, which are the producers of our thoughts about Christianity, can be called into question just as readily as psychological methods. Each is subject to the biasing effects of its own professional orthodoxy. For example, the power structure of the theology profession can easily dictate how theology is to be done and who is allowed to do it. Theology can officially become the sole province of one race and one sex with one very limited way of doing things. In chapter 2, then, the question will be *Should theological methods be examined before facts that they produce are integrated?*

The next integration issue concerns the methodology of the

actual integration procedure itself. For some Christians, the procedure is simply a matter of making the Bible the central core of truth around which psychology must function and against which it must be tested. This creates an immediate tension in the integration process, although to evangelical Christians it seems the only right and proper thing to do.

Upon closer inspection, it can be seen that the Bible and psychology are really in two different categories. The Bible is an object that we study, and psychology is a way that we study objects. It would be more accurate to say—and what is really happening is—that psychology (a way of studying people) is being subsumed under the authority of theology (a way of studying the Bible). That raises the question, Should one discipline (psychology) be "under" another (theology)? And, by implication, Is it imperative that one discipline must keep the other disciplines in line? The issue is: *Should theology be the guardian discipline for protecting the truth?* This will be discussed in chapter 3.

Another issue that confronts us when we take a close look at the integration process has to do with the nature of truth. Many Christians believe that there are different degrees of truth that can be integrated. For example, we have "disclosed" truth in the Bible and "discovered" truth in nature.[13] The implication is that truth disclosed to the theologian reading the Bible is truer than truth discovered by the psychologist studying people. It appears that Truth is being distinguished from mere truth.[14] *Can one truth be truer than another?* is one question dealt with in chapter 4.

Closely associated with the nature of truth is the nature of the data that contain the truths to be integrated. There is a bit of confusion, first of all, regarding just what data are. Some Christian psychologists equate data with facts.[15] The term "data," however, refers to a level of reality that precedes facts. Facts are interpretations of data. As such, facts are vulnerable to personal subjectivity—they are theory laden—in a way that raw data are not.[16]

The logical conclusion is that the data base is privileged, but the interpretations are not. For example, the Bible itself has priority over theological facts derived from the Bible. Assuming this to be the case, we can further conclude that theological *facts* are not necessarily superior to any other kind of facts (e.g., psychological facts). What we must not conclude, however, is that all data bases are on a par. The Bible stands alone. It occupies a special position in God's revelation of truth through his creation. In other words, biblical *data* are privileged (or sacred, according to Christian anthropologist Charles Kraft)[17] in comparison with all other kinds of data—such as data generated by human subjects in a psychological experiment.

What are we to say, then, about the *process* of deducing the facts from the data? Does the privileged position of the Bible mean that the process of discerning truth in Scripture is fundamentally different from the process of understanding truth elsewhere in creation? We need to ask, *How does God reveal his truths through the biblical data studied by theologians as compared with the personal data studied by psychologists?* That will be the second issue dealt with in chapter 4.

The biggest integration issue of all is probably the balance between thought and application. Integration is often nothing more than an intellectual exercise. There frequently seems to be an overabundance of theory and a shortage of action. Lots of words, very few deeds. Much talk, not much walk.

It reminds me of what happens in corporate worship. All too often worship becomes a cerebral activity devoid of any physical activity that would give expression to our thoughts. However, according to well-known author Richard Foster:

> Worship that is solely cerebral is an aberration. . . .
>
> The Bible describes worship in physical terms. The root meaning for the Hebrew word we translate *worship* is "to prostrate." The word *bless* literally means "to kneel." *Thanksgiving* refers to "an extension of the hand." Throughout Scripture we find a variety of physical postures in connection with worship. . . .
>
> We are to present our bodies to God in worship in a posture consistent with the inner spirit in worship. Standing, clapping, dancing, lifting the hands, lifting the head are postures consistent with the spirit of praise. . . . Kneeling, bowing the head, lying prostrate are postures consistent with the spirit of humility. . . . The . . .

> question is "what kind of worship does God call for?" It is clear that God calls for wholehearted worship.[18]

It is clear to me that God is also calling for wholehearted integration. Not just God-talk but God-walk. I would have to say, however, that the few integration approaches that have ventured beyond the "solely cerebral" have ended up being only half-hearted.

One such approach is that proposed by several Christian psychologists at the Rosemead School of Psychology at Biola University. Their idea of integration is to think Christianly about psychology and psychologically about Christianity and then proceed toward either an abstract collection of those thoughts or a concretely lived personal experience. They claim that the three components of the procedure are not isolated from one another but form a dynamic whole.[19]

It seems to me that just the opposite is the case. The two alternatives are to move from those individual concepts that are common to both psychology and Christianity to a more broadly conceived collection of concepts *or* to concrete lived experience. The two alternatives are therefore not directly related to each other. They are, in fact, held in isolation with each being a completion of the integration process in its own right.

A further problem develops when we look more closely at the lived experience level of the proposal. It is quite obvious that lived experience does not actually complete the integration process; it runs parallel to it.[20] Lived experience refers to a way of living that encourages openness to God working in our lives and also awareness of our biases so that we do not shut ourselves off from certain sources of truth or from other perspectives. We should be nondefensive, humble, tolerant of ambiguity, balanced in the expression of our thoughts and feelings, and committed to God. This sounds to me like the description of an integrated person, not an integration process.

Lived experience must be included directly in the process of integration through the application of the results of thinking integrative thoughts. That is what makes integration truly a dynamic whole.

Is integration ever whole, or complete, when it is only intellectual? And if personally lived experience is brought in, is it seen as the natural and necessary completion of the integration process? These are the questions that should be asked of every integrative approach. Talking *and* walking, that is what wholehearted integration is all about. And that means talking through the inert data and facts with the living God. Talking and walking with God is the theme that unites Christianity and psychology and that unites the chapters of this book.

Chapters 1 and 2 concern talking with God in the disciplines of psychology and theology. In integrating psychology and Christianity, these are the methods that allow us to talk with God to discover the truths that he reveals to us through his general and special revelations. And those are the truths that we will want to introduce into our daily lives—into our daily walk with the Author of all truth. Chapter 1 is a detailed analysis of the present state of affairs in psychology and of how it might be improved to allow for more of the activity of God in the conduct of psychological research. In other words, the initial chapter proposes how we might talk more directly with God through the discipline of psychology. Chapter 2 asks some further questions: Who is doing theology? How is theology done? How can religious experience be studied and validated as direct communication from God? Again, the purpose is to suggest how to talk more directly with God—in this case through the discipline of theology.

Chapter 3 is the core of our exploration. Here is where talking with God and walking with God come together. Two alternative integration methodologies are presented. One emphasizes talking about talking with God; the other emphasizes walking with God. The two alternatives, critical integration and embodied integration, are presented and contrasted in detail. The conclusion is that integration should be balanced and incarnational; that is, it should move from comparison of psychological and theological concepts, through clarification of Christian thought regarding those concepts, into personal conviction and commitment to action. It should entail following Jesus wholeheartedly in both word and deed, allowing God's truth to live through us as we live as Jesus lived.

The final chapter is about truth, the Bible, and the person. Though it is the foundational chapter, I have good reason for not putting it at the beginning. Perhaps the most natural ordering would have been: (1) truth, the Bible, and the person, (2) theology, (3) psychology, and (4) integration methodology. However, in my estimation, the chief problem area in integration today concerns methodology. Nowhere in the literature can we find adequate guidelines for doing psychology in such a way that the quality of integration is enhanced, or guidelines for doing theology with an eye toward improving our integration efforts, or guidelines for how to do integration itself. This book attempts to provide that. Therefore, it is important to show the reader right from the beginning that this is a how-to book, by starting with the methodological concerns of and guidelines for the disciplines of psychology and theology and proceeding nonstop through to the conclusion of alternative guidelines for the process of integration.

After completing the priority discussion of methodological guidelines, it is important that we step back and look at the nature of the objects of the methods. The common object of all the methods (psychological, theological, and integrative), of course, is truth. In chapter 4 we will see that the nature of truth is inseparable from the nature of knowing truth, which is always a mixture of subjective and objective factors. We will also see that truth exists in spite of us and demands our response. It is our response, or commitment through action, that completes the process of knowing truth. This will easily be recognized as the biblical process of knowing truth. In Scripture, knowledge of the truth is comprised of intellectual understanding plus experiential knowledge, or talking with God plus walking with God.

The Bible and the person are the distinct objects of the methods of theology and psychology, respectively. They are therefore important individual topics in chapter 4. The Bible is described as having a dual nature, owing to the fact that it is part human and part divine. In addition, the Bible's authority is determined to be based, not solely on an a priori doctrinal statement about Scripture, but on Spirit-led subjection to Scripture itself. The nature of the person is also described as involving relationship with God, because we are created in God's image and with the capacity to be indwelled by the Holy Spirit. Therefore, the essence of both the Bible and the person is determined by relationship of the human and the divine. Both are, by nature, ready for the dialogue with God that is possible via the methods described in chapters 1 and 2. The foundation is ready for wholehearted integration.

Notes

1. Meyer, D. *The positive thinkers: Religion as pop psychology from Mary Baker Eddy to Oral Roberts,* 2d ed. New York: Pantheon Books, 1980.

2. Peale, N. V. *You can win*. Nashville: Abingdon, 1938, p. 79.

3. Shostrom, E. L., & Montgomery, D. *Healing love: How God works within the personality*. Nashville: Abingdon, 1978.

4. Ludwig, T. E.; Westphal, M.; Klay, R. J.; and Myers, D. G. *Inflation, poortalk, and the Gospel*. Valley Forge, Pa.: Judson, 1981.

5. Ibid., pp. 69–70.

6. Frank, J. D. Nature and functions of belief systems: Humanism and transcendental religion. *American Psychologist* 32 (1977): 555–59.

7. Collins, G. R. *Psychology and theology: Prospects for integration*. Nashville: Abingdon, 1981, pp. 19–20; Everett, W. W., and Bachmeyer, T. J. *Disciplines in transformation: A guide to theology and the behavioral sciences.* Washington, D.C.: University Press of America, 1979 chap. 9.

8. Koch, S. Language communities, search cells, and the psychological studies. In *Nebraska Symposium on Motivation 1975,* ed. J. K. Cole and W. J. Arnold. Lincoln: University of Nebraska, 1976, pp. 477–559.

9. Ellens, J. H. Biblical themes in psychological theory and practice. *The CAPS Bulletin* 6(2) (1980): 2–6.

10. Carter, J. D., and Narramore, B. *The integration of psychology and theology: An introduction.* Grand Rapids: Zondervan, 1979 chap. 1.

11. Fleck, J. R., and Carter, J. D. eds., *Psychology and Christianity: Integrative readings.* Nashville: Abingdon, 1981.

12. Collins, G. R. *The rebuilding of psychology: An integration of psychology and Christianity.* Wheaton: Tyndale House, 1977 chap. 8.

13. Collins, *Psychology and theology,* p. 35.

14. Glasser, A. F. Integration is impossible if God speaks with two voices, excerpted in Collins, *Psychology and theology,* pp. 86–94.

15. Fleck and Carter, *Psychology and Christianity,* pp. 17–18.

16. DeVries, M. J. Beyond integration: New directions. *The CAPS Bulletin* 7(3) (1981): 1–5.

17. Kraft, C. H. Can anthropological insight assist evangelical theology? *Christian Scholar's Review* 7 (1977): 165–202.

18. Foster, R. J. *Celebration of discipline: The path to spiritual growth.* New York: Harper & Row, 1978, pp. 146–47.

19. Fleck and Carter, *Psychology and Christianity,* pp. 19–21.

20. See Carter and Narramore, *Integration,* chap. 8.

1

Psychology

Change is in the air. Many psychologists are calling for an entirely new research paradigm in psychology, or at least a change in emphasis from an almost totally exclusive reliance on experimental methodology. Some are even advocating surgery that would be radical enough to produce a "Christian psychology," or at least a psychology that would be more compatible with biblical principles.

I am generally supportive of such correctives and am most particularly in agreement with making psychology less experimental and more Christian. However, there is no reason to think that experimental psychology cannot be considered Christian. My point is that, on the one hand, I favor alternative methods for studying persons, and, on the other hand, I support attempts to make all psychological research methods as congruent with Christianity as possible.

Several Christian psychologists have recently expressed similar convictions; among them Collins, Koteskey, and Van Leeuwen with proposals to rebuild,[1] reinterpret,[2] and reform[3] psychology. They all believe that psychology is badly fragmented and therefore in need of fundamental reconstruction, and that any basic changes in the discipline of psychology can and should be done from a Christian perspective.

My question is How would basic changes in the psychological component affect the overall quality of integration? Would a transformed psychology help us talk more directly with God and thereby enhance the quality of integration? Let us turn first to the question of whether the integration process could benefit from changes in the discipline of psychology, then why psychology needs to be fundamentally changed and what direction change should take, and finally how the recommended changes would enhance the quality of integration.

The Need for Change

Since our main topic is integration, any discussion of the need for change within psychology must relate, not just to what is best for psychology, but also to what is best for integration. Within that context, we need to consider how the quality of psychology affects the quality of integration.

Most people would agree that integration is not merely an abstract, intellectual, playing-with-ideas game, and, most certainly, the ideas that are involved are not fluffy-headed intellectualizations but are grounded in reality. This valid grounding depends on the psychological and theological methodologies that are involved. Some of the ideas or concepts may seem pretty abstract, but they refer to concrete reality as determined by the research methods that produced them. The validity or truthfulness of the concepts being integrated is therefore totally dependent on the adequacy of those research methods.

The entire integration process will sink or swim depending upon what might be called the methodological starting point. Integration is only as valid as the concepts being related, and the concepts are only as valid as the research that produces them. It all starts at the research level. That is why the quality of integration is directly affected by the quality of the research methods. Therefore, if the quality of psychology is improved, so is the quality of integration.

In order to improve our efforts at integration, what evidence can be found that psychology needs to change in some significant ways?

Every research methodology arises out of a set of assumptions that helps determine the course the research will take. In psychology there are several assumptions that guide most investigations. Two in particular—two ideological faith commitments—must be examined.

Evolutionism and Behaviorism

The first ideology is evolutionism. This theoretical system begins with the assumption that humans evolved from lower animals. The comparative research that results is based on the observed similarities across species of anatomical structures and physiological functions. But then all kinds of problems arise when it is further assumed that behavioral processes are also alike. Psychologists have gotten a lot of mileage out of speculating about the comparability of the thoughts and feelings of monkeys and the thoughts and feelings of men. Such a degree of continuity between humans and lower forms of animal life, however, is at least not reconcilable from a biblical perspective.[4]

The other ideology is behaviorism. Included in its articles of faith is a strong commitment to the identifying characteristics of the natural sciences—laboratories, impersonal procedures, measurements—to the exclusion of naturalistic observation, personal interaction, and meanings. Also included by behavioristic psychologists, as an added feature, is deception about the real nature of the research. This deception further precludes the possibility of meaningful dialogue between any two persons involved in the research.

Behaviorism is also committed to belief in the infinite malleability of the human person. Thus, all problems are seen as social ones that will disappear when the social environment is properly manipulated. This is the quintessence of B. F. Skinner's social vision. Another example of the behavioristic passion for environmental explanations is attribution theory's exaggerated emphasis on situational factors in explaining why people behave as they do.

In a nutshell, psychology is committed, as a natural science, to measurement rather than meaning, to correlation rather than intention. However, "If psychology has a bible, it is the statistical textbook, but many students shy away from psychology's scriptures, preferring Freudian to Cartesian projection, moral values to eigenvalues, human frontiers to statistical limits."[5] And "With regard to the importance of *meaning,* we need to go no further than the Decalogue and the Sermon on the Mount, both of which refer not only to actions themselves (e.g., adultery, murder, theft), but also to the importance of the meaning behind the actions (e.g., lust, hate, covetousness)."[6]

Psychology is also committed to deception rather than dialogue. Let us pursue that further.

Deception

The necessity of deception in psychological research must be challenged. For years the professional orthodoxy has been the assumption that first-person information cannot be trusted as much as third-person information. People in general are just not capable of giving accurate, unbiased accounts of their own experience. They do not know themselves well enough to be accurate and are too defensive to be unbiased. Self-report cannot be trusted, so people must be deceived in order to discover their real thoughts. And in order to deceive, the researcher must remain detached, peeping at people through keyholes rather than interacting with them as persons.[7] I believe that assuming we can automatically know people through detached, devious methods better than they know themselves leads to the myth of "immaculate perception" and to professional arrogance.

Deception became standard operating procedure during the 1960s. Psychologist Zick Rubin reports that

> to study social behavior "scientifically," researchers created trumped-up situations and then observed their subjects' reactions.

> To explore the impact of self-esteem on behavior, for example, researchers gave subjects glowing or damning "reports" on their maturity. To investigate the effects of guilt, they told subjects that they had broken a piece of equipment.[8]

Today, such trickery is still flourishing. Stooges are posing as fellow subjects but secretly following prearranged scripts, subjects are being given false reports about "test" results, and on and on it goes. Deception, according to Rubin, is just being taken for granted. One of the biggest reasons is probably the confidence that researchers have in the debriefing session after an experiment is completed. This is done supposedly for the educational benefit and emotional welfare of the subject.

I think it is at least partially accurate, however, to say that debriefing often becomes an indoctrination session in which the subject is led to believe that the experiment has actually been an educational experience. On other occasions, it may become little more than an attempt to assuage the experimenter's guilt over having possibly hurt the subject in some way or having required a student to spend time in an experiment as a course requirement (the requirement often derives as much from the experimenter's need for a subject pool as it does from the student's need for hands-on learning). All things considered, I do not believe that the possible harm from deception and the mixed benefits from debriefing are an even trade-off.

The answer to the problems associated with deceiving and debriefing is not to work harder to come up with newer and more effective deception studies and debriefing procedures. Rather, we should work harder at helping people to know themselves as truthfully as possible and to communicate that understanding to others as accurately as possible. We need to do our research so that it builds trust, not mistrust (of people in general and psychologists in particular). We need to stop lying and start "looking at social behavior as it actually occurs."[9]

To encourage further thought on this topic, I recommend additional reading in the psychological literature[10] as well as the Christian literature.[11]

A Critique of Psychology as a Natural Science

The centerpiece of psychology as a natural science is the experiment. A peculiar fact about psychological experiments, however, is that their outcomes are almost always completely anticipated beforehand. Thus, they are more involved with demonstration than with discovery.[12] If an experiment does not turn out "right," the experimenter does not conclude that the hypothesis might be wrong. Rather, the methodology is corrected and revised until the phenomenon of interest can at last be demonstrated.

> But note that what the experiment tests is not whether the hypothesis is true but rather whether the experimenter is a sufficiently ingenious stage manager to produce in the laboratory conditions which demonstrate that an obviously true hypothesis is correct.[13]

It is often a letdown for students in psychology to learn that experiments are basically demonstrations. Psychology loses its air of excitement; the mystery is gone, and all that is left is an emphasis on mastery. In spite of this understandable reaction, there is more that needs to be said.

The Six R's of Psychological Research

Through the years, as I have taught psychology courses and kept up with the professional literature, I have noticed five characteristics of psychology as a natural science: reductionism, rigor, rigidity, replication, and ratomorphism. These always seem to be in a state of tension with the identifying characteristic of psychology as a more human science—relevance. I consider the six characteristics the six R's of psychological research and submit that research is always a trade-off between any one or combination of the first five and the sixth.

Reductionism

Any scientific investigation must reduce a large amount of data down to a smaller, more manageable amount during the analysis phase that is designed to get at the truth of the matter that is being investigated. Scientific reduction is entirely appropriate. Reduction*ism,* however, is not. This is the assumption that reduction should take place *before* the data are collected, as well as afterward as a part of the data analysis process. It is the initial assumption that complex psychological processes—indeed entire persons—are best studied in the simplest terms possible.

Consequently, stimulus-response connections are seen as the way to understand emotions, and cognitions are likened to computer programs. Persons are referred to as machines, which makes them easier to study. In fact, we hear that "man is nothing but a machine," and we read that humans are nothing but "naked apes." Assertions such as these have been refuted often, still "nothingbutism" continues to rear its ugly head.[14]

Reductionism is taking a toll in broad cultural terms as well as in the education of students in psychology. Well-known psychologist Nevitt Sanford warns that psychology is changing the world far less by its research findings than by the image of human beings that guides the research.[15] It is that image that deeply affects the self-images of the individual consumers of psychology. Former president of the American Psychological Association, Donald Campbell, is alarmed that psychology is recruiting students into its ranks who are overeager to adopt a view of persons that is simplistic and mechanistic.[16] As Campbell points out, it is not hard to imagine what effects such deliberate initial oversimplification has on the research findings that are eventually produced by those students.

Reductionistic research can be useful, but we are obliged to remember its limitations. I can take a piece of chalk and break it, and I will have two pieces of chalk. I can cut a worm in two, and it will leave in two directions. But half a person is not a person at all!

Rigor

There is a tendency in psychology to strive to make research studies clean and neat. Precision, or rigor, is the ideal state aspired to in the well-designed experiment, even when it is at the expense of overall significance.

Organizational psychologist Chris Argyris has discovered some unintended consequences of a heavy reliance on rigorous research by relating the properties of "well-designed" research to the properties of formal organizations. They are remarkably similar. "Rigorousness is to a researcher what efficiency is to an executive. . . . Moreover, many of the dysfunctions reported between experimenter and subject are similar to the dysfunctions between management and employee."[17]

Argyris arrived at his rather interesting conclusion by initially summarizing the criteria for conducting rigorous research. First is the removal of ambiguity from the problem being investigated and from the relevant variables. The emphasis is on ease of observing and measuring the variables. Second is maximum control by the researcher over those variables. He then found that where behavior is tightly defined, controlled, and evaluated, conditions are created for the subject that are similar to "the most mechanized assembly-line conditions." Argyris was then able to observe that, because of the close similarity between the conditions in organizations and the conditions in rigorous research, the same unintended consequences caused by the former can be connected to the latter. They include, in the language of research, such things as "psychological withdrawal while remaining physically in the research situation . . . knowingly giving incorrect answers, being a difficult subject, second-guessing the research design and trying to circumvent it in some fashion, producing the minimally accepted amount of behavior, coercing others to produce minimally, and disbelief and mistrust of the researcher."[18]

Rigor is not such an ideal state after all. It certainly is not worth aspiring to at the expense of significance. In fact, in the interest of significance, I would say that if research is not really worth doing, then it is not worth doing well.

Rigidity

When our desire to be rigorous becomes so strong that we will consider only one method (e.g., the experiment) for our research, regardless of the problem we want to investigate, we are being very rigid. Such rigidity is a bias—a method bias—that allows us to ask only those questions that can be answered using our favorite method. It is like saying that if something cannot be measured it is not meaningful.

To allow our methods to dictate the questions we ask is to be like the person whose only tool was a hammer, so he treated everything as if it were a nail. In a word, it is rigorism, or rigor mortis.

A rigid approach can succeed at times, but we must remember its limitations. If my research is guided more by how *easy* I can make it using the method I am good at than by how *important* I can make it using a more appropriate method, I will not succeed very often. Philosopher Abraham Kaplan calls this the law of the instrument.[19] It reminds me of the story about the drunkard who was searching under a street lamp for his keys, which he had dropped on the other side of the street. Asked why he was looking for his keys on this side under the lamppost, he replied, "It's lighter here!"

Replication

One of the standard operating procedures of psychology as a natural science is replication, or the repeating of a study by independent researchers. This procedure is an accepted validation tool and an excellent tool for teaching methodology.

However, it can easily become a tool for overemphasis on prediction and control and deemphasis on discovery—mastery rather than mystery. This mystery/mastery tension is aptly described by psychologist David Bakan.

> One is tempted to think that psychologists are often like children playing cowboys. When children play cowboys they emulate them in everything but their main work, which is taking care of cows. The main work of the scientist is thinking and making discoveries of what was not thought of beforehand. Psychologists often attempt to "play scientist" by avoiding the main work.[20]

The imbalance of mastery and mystery in contemporary psychology bothers me. I think it also bothered another writer who believes we live from bottle to basket, cradle to casket, on a learner's permit. The tragedy is that much of what we learn is a false certainty pasted over the deeper ambiguities of existence."[21] That is, mastery pasted over mystery!

Ratomorphism

"Ratomorphism" is a clever name for arguing through analogy with animals. In other words, the same label is attached to human and, let us say, rat behaviors that look similar. And if the rat behaviors are thoroughly understood, then it is claimed that the human behaviors can be explained in the same way. Thus, scientists have shown that certain animals stake out an area and protect it, because of their territorial instinct. So if I take a shotgun after someone who drives a car all over my lawn, it is because of my . . . territorial instinct.[22]

The problem with this practice in psychology is that although analogies sound plausible, they have only their plausibility for support. And if either side of the analogy is challenged, another analogy will be forthcoming; several challenges will simply result in a matching number of new analogies.

The other side of ratomorphism is to reverse the analogy and attribute human qualities to animals. I can remember reading reports in popular magazines, for example, of research trumpeting the conclusion that rats fed marijuana extract became "depressed." Even more surprising is to read in a reputable professional journal an account by Harry Harlow, former president of the American Psychological Association, of inducing "psychopathology" in rhesus monkeys by isolating them until they became "depressed." During prolonged periods of separation from their mothers, "young monkeys ceased their peer play activity and became withdrawn and inactive." This was termed "depressive behavior," or "depressive withdrawal." In another study, a vertical chamber apparatus was utilized. "Depression in humans has been characterized as a state of 'helplessness and hopelessness, sunken in a well of despair', and the chambers were designed to reproduce such a well for monkey subjects." The result of confinement in the chambers for even a relatively short period of time was "profound and prolonged depression" in the monkeys.[23]

Harlow's results raise serious questions. Is "monkey depression" really the same as a human person's experience of what it is like to be depressed? Is the desolate human experience referred to as a well of despair at all comparable to what it is like for a monkey to be confined, literally, in a well?

Relevance

This is the other side of the trade-off and is represented by the positive pole of the contrasts within each of the five characteristics of psychology as a natural science. In other words, relevance is the preference for complexity over nothingbutism—reductionism, for significance over precision—rigor, for importance over ease—rigidity, for mystery over mastery—replication, and for the truly human over the merely animal—ratomorphism.

Relevance is the primary consideration of psychology as a human science. However, since psychology has been so thoroughly impregnated by the natural-science orientation, relevance is not yet the rallying cry it should be. The one-sided trade-off is beautifully portrayed by popular psychologist Rollo May's lighthearted but accurate fantasy about a deceased psychologist trying to get into heaven.

> A psychologist—any psychologist, or all of us—arrives at the heavenly gates at the end of his long and productive life. He is brought up before St. Peter for the customary accounting. Formidable, St. Peter sits calmly behind his table looking like the Moses of Michelangelo. An angel assistant in a white jacket drops a manila folder on the table which St. Peter opens and looks at, frowning. Despite the awesome visage of the judge, the psychologist clutches his briefcase and steps up with commendable courage.
>
> But St. Peter's frown deepens. He drums with his fingers on the table and grunts a few nondirective "uhm-uhm"s as he fixes the candidate with his Mosaic eyes.
>
> The silence is discomfiting. Finally the psychologist opens his briefcase and cries, "Here! The reprints of my hundred and thirty-two papers."
>
> St. Peter slowly shakes his head. . . .
>
> At last St. Peter speaks. "I'm aware, my good man, how industrious you were. It's not sloth you're accused of. Nor is it unscientific behavior." Falling into silence again, his brow becomes darker. . . .
>
> "Well, it's true," [the psychologist] admits with a fine show of frankness, "I did twist the data a bit on my Ph.D. research."

But St. Peter will not be placated. "No," he says, . . . "it's not immorality. . . . You're as ethical as the next man. Nor am I accusing you of being a behaviorist or a mystic or a functionalist or an existentialist or a Rogerian. Those are only minor sins."

Now St. Peter slaps his hand resoundingly down on the table, and his tone is like Moses breaking the news of the ten commandments: . . .

"You have spent your life making molehills out of mountains—that's what you're guilty of. When man was tragic, you made him trivial. . . . When . . . he drummed up enough courage to act, you called it stimulus and response. Man had passion; and when you were pompous and lecturing to your class you called it 'the satisfaction of basic needs,' and when you were relaxed and looking at your secretary you called it 'release of tension.' You made man over into the image of your childhood Erector Set or Sunday School maxims. . . .

"In short, we sent you . . . to a Dantean circus, and you spent your days and nights at sideshows!"[24]

The judgment of psychology as a natural science is quite harsh, and Christian psychologists are beginning to join the chorus. Mary Van Leeuwen, for example, is arguing that psychology as a natural science is neither successful nor ethically acceptable. Briefly, her argument is that promises of a "thorough and reliable understanding of human psychological processes" have not been kept because of significant limitations on reliability and exportability of research findings and inattention to "many specifically human concerns which cannot be quantified, operationalized or manipulated." When the unfulfilled promises are combined with grave ethical concerns regarding the "routine use of deception and the infliction of some sort of temporary distress," it is a clear signal of the need for change.[25]

It should be quite clear from all I have said that psychology needs to incorporate some of the features of a more humane perspective. In addition, it needs to develop an alternate methodology based on a completely humanistic orientation (by "humanistic" I mean respect and concern for the human person, not the ideology of secular humanism). What would a human-science orientation involve?

A Description of Psychology as a Human Science

The first question that needs to be answered is What is a human science? What are some of its characteristics?

Van Leeuwen lists the main features of a human-science orientation:

1. A holistic view of "mental life as the total reaction of the thinking, feeling, striving self to a situation confronting it."
2. Recognition that "all human phenomena are contextual—that is, embedded in an ongoing spatial and temporal milieu which gives them meaning and hence must be taken into account."
3. An understanding of "phenomena on their own terms and for their own sake, without regard to what causes them or how they can be used to cause something else."
4. Tolerance of ambiguity—that is, living with "the realization that the essence of any situation or the human response to it cannot adequately be captured in cookbook terms allowing for facile replication elsewhere."
5. A careful spelling out of the researcher's biases before conducting the research and allowing them to "inform the conduct of [the] research and its subsequent write-up."
6. Disclosure of the true purpose of the research to all the participants, who are "regarded as collaborators in the entire enterprise."
7. The "use of a descriptive, qualitative methodology."
8. The employment of "active dialog between the researcher and those researched."[26]

It is possible that an all-out attempt to develop psychology along these lines has been somewhat delayed by cognitive psychology, the currently fashionable approach to the study of how people perceive, remember, and think. Those with humanistic leanings can easily get caught up in the excitement of legitimately studying human thought processes. For many it is a refreshing change from the more sterile topics that seem to make up the major portion of psychology's agenda. Ulric Neisser, the acknowledged father of cognitive psychology, warns that it is usually just more of the same, however—merely a diversion.

> Most experimental cognitive psychology has taken a narrowly academic view of human abilities. The subjects of most experiments are given very artificial test-like tasks. They might be asked to report how many dots appeared, or classify characters, or say whether two forms are identical or not. They are *not* supposed to get bored, wonder whether the experiment is worth doing, respond for their own amusement, or quit. Yet often these would be intelligent courses of action. . . .
>
> The prevailing view in [cognitive] psychology is usually one that is most convenient for us and least convenient for the people we theorize about. Psychologists rubricize people—put them into categories. They reduce mental processes to the simplest possible terms. They say, it's all association, or it's all conditioning, or it's all X, where X is whatever the current psychological fashion dictates. Whatever X may be, and whatever good experiments may originally have determined X, it does serious injustice to any person who is thinking and acting and moving and feeling in the real world. . . . You've got to listen to how people say it is.[27]

There have been several isolated attempts to incorporate some of the characteristics of a human science into psychology. A few psychologists have utilized human-science oriented methods as a preliminary step in generating hypotheses to be tested later experimentally. Robert MacLeod in particular championed this approach.[28]

Others have developed human-science oriented procedures as correctives to the experiment itself. The most radical corrective is to take the entire psychological study out of the laboratory—removing manipulation from the methodology—as a supplementary field test for the laboratory findings. This is a type of "naturalistic observation."[29]

One well-known problem to which correctives have been applied is the persistent finding that the personality of the researcher can be a biasing factor in an experiment.[30] Bakan points out that the personality type of the experimenter can be the determining factor in choosing a statistical test of significance, which will inadvertently bias the results.[31] And Harvard psychologist Robert Rosenthal warns of experimenter bias, or the unintended communication to subjects by supposedly neutral, uninvolved experimenters of expectations regarding the outcome of the experiment.[32] In both cases, awareness of the potential problem can serve in and of itself as a corrective, although Rosenthal also proposes detailed correctives for the expectancy problem.

Another problem concerns the fact that subjects often respond more to personal agenda and environmental distractions in the experimental situation than to the verbatim instructions. For example, subjects enact a wide variety of roles based on their preconceptions, motives, and suspicions. Thus, we have "good" subjects (who want to help the experimenter), "faithful" subjects (who want to do good science), "apprehensive" subjects (who are uptight about being evaluated), "negativistic" subjects (whom I call "dirty rats"),[33] "enlightened" subjects (who want to be accurately represented),[34] and a host of others.

In addition, subjects are affected by "demand characteristics," or environmental cues that create compelling expectations and demands. Hypnosis researcher Martin Orne recommends a human-science oriented, double corrective of the "preexperimental inquiry" and "postexperimental interview" to combat the problem of role enactments as well as that of demand characteristics.[35]

Currently, the most completely developed human-science orientation in psychology is phenomenological psychology. Having taught a course in this approach for the past ten years, I am quite familiar with its concepts and methodology. Basically, it is an attitude as well as an approach. It is an attitude of respect for the dignity and integrity of personal experience. It is also an approach or method for studying, without fear or favor, the meaning of lived experience. The context for such study is collaboration and trust rather than manipulation and deception. The result of a phenomenological study is a qualitative description of the personal meaning of lived experience. This differs significantly in content as well as form from the results of natural-science oriented research:

quantitative analyses of impersonal measurements of observed behaviors.

A distinction must be made between phenomenological psychology and phenomenological philosophy, even though they have many similarities and common inheritances. The most obvious difference is in the focus of their research. Typically, philosophical research focuses on self-reflection, while psychological research focuses on interpersonal dialogue.[36]

Psychologists Henryk Misiak and Virginia Staudt Sexton have compiled an excellent survey of the development of the psychological side of the phenomenological movement, as has philosopher Herbert Spiegelberg.[37] Of particular note are the first contribution of a systematic phenomenological approach to the American psychological literature by psychologists Donald Snygg and Arthur Combs and the first major American symposium on phenomenological psychology—with such notable participants as psychologists Sigmund Koch, Robert MacLeod, Carl Rogers, and B. F. Skinner.[38]

Also noteworthy is the emergence of the psychology department at Duquesne University in Pittsburgh. Psychologists at Duquesne and several of their graduates have made diverse and substantial contributions to the growing literature in phenomenological psychology. Most notable are the four volumes of the *Duquesne Studies in Phenomenological Psychology* and Amedeo Giorgi's *Psychology as a Human Science*.[39] In addition, the highly successful *Journal of Phenomenological Psychology* was founded in 1971 at Duquesne.

Phenomenological Psychology: The Concepts

There have been several attempts to list the central concepts of phenomenological psychology. Among the clearest are the works of French phenomenologist Maurice Merleau-Ponty and Giorgi.[40] A complete listing of major concepts would have to include at least the following:

Description

A phenomenological study aims basically to describe rather than explain, to understand how rather than why. The goal is to provide reliable guideposts for others to be able to understand their own, similar experience. Applied in a Christian context, personal testimonies, for example, would provide guideposts to help others better understand their own experience of God.

C. S. Lewis must have had something of this sort in mind when he said:

> The kind of explanation which explains things away may give us something, though at a heavy cost. But you cannot go on "explaining away" for ever: you will find that you have explained explanation itself away. You cannot go on "seeing through" things forever. The whole point of seeing through something is to see something through it. It is good that the window should be transparent, because the street or garden beyond it is opaque. How if you saw through the garden too? . . . If you see through everything, then everything is transparent. But a wholly transparent world is an invisible world. To "see through" all things is the same as not to see.[41]

The purpose of a phenomenological investigation is to describe lived experience well enough so that others might see themselves through it, as when they read a good novel. The novel most certainly, however, would not explain the experience away as nothing but . . . .

Co-investigation

A phenomenological investigation is a *co*-investigation, a collaborative dialogue between two people trying to understand an experience as lived by one of them. The people involved are referred to as investigator and co-investigator, rather than experimenter and subject. The job of the investigator is to understand, that is, stand under (feel the weight of), the experience in the co-investigator's terms. The co-investigator is a true partner in the research enterprise, rather than a subject in the control of the investigator.

The goal of the co-investigation is to *use* the subjectivity of the co-investigator rather than try to control it. Personal impressions are not treated as contamination that must be kept out of the study. The co-investigator is not viewed as a passive respondent, and the investigator is not merely a detached observer. Rather, the co-investigator is seen as an active participant in a process in which the investigator is also very much involved.

Bracketing

In order for a phenomenological description to be faithful to what the co-investigator has actually experienced, instead of what perhaps "should" have been experienced, the investigator needs to temporarily leave aside ("bracket") questions of reality, truth, and cause, and any other personal biases. This does not involve valueless tolerance, but it does involve tolerance of ambiguity. In other words, can the investigator stand not knowing something about the co-investigator's experience "for sure" or not letting the co-investigator know the "real" truth about the experience or suggesting what caused it? Can the investigator temporarily leave aside what he or she knows will impede the co-investigator's revelation of the actual experience?

Meaning

A phenomenological description is a detailed account of what a particular experience means to the co-investigator. In other words, it portrays the significance or value of the experience for the co-investigator, plus the details of what it was like, or what it felt like. For example:

> What is it to make something? I knew this clay before it was born—when it was nothing, just a special kind of dirt. I wedged it so that it became even and smooth, without air bubbles—a consistent something, and not just a chunk torn from a bigger chunk. I put it on the wheel and put the wheel in motion, and with a steady pressure of my hands brought the clay into roundness. My fingers made a well in the center, and my left hand went inside and pulled over toward my right hand to make the base. The two hands together squeezed the clay and pulled it up into a cylinder, a simple

form. . . . The clay passed through several transitory shapes on the theme of a single curve. I experienced a kind of impatience, a wish to choose. Finally, I liked the shape. It was apparent that the choice was a victory of the need to choose, to settle on something, over the need to experience something new. . . . I took the pot off the wheel and set it aside. The next day, when it was firm enough, I trimmed away the excess clay. I trimmed too much; some of the vitality of the pot was sacrificed to a superficial sophistication of form. The pot was put to dry. Weeks later, it was fired. The fired pot was "pleasant," I told myself. . . . I glazed the pot and fired it again. When I took it out of the kiln and the pot was new to me, I realized that the lip was weak, that the curve was far from subtle. The pot was very light. . . .

I don't know how I feel about the pot, and the discomfort of this moment is very like the discomfort of searching for form on the wheel. I sense that in the need to decide whether I'm pleased or displeased with the pot, pleased or displeased with the way I worked at making it, pleased or displeased with myself as a potter and as a person, that in this either/or, I close myself off from the living wholeness of experience. But the moment passes, and I decide it's a decent pot with some not-too-obvious flaws.

For me, that is what it's like to work at a craft: that is what really takes place. . . .

When I speak to people about what I do and what pottery is for me, . . . over the years, some of the luster has faded from the picture. . . .

It became increasingly clear that I worked at pottery exactly the way I did everything else. . . . When I saw that I made the same few forms in pottery again and again, I tried to change the form by working harder at shaping the pot. Gradually, I became aware that the pot was a reflection of my inadequate and false self-image. If, for example, I see myself as a direct and forthright person, I will make sturdy pots with simple straight sides—what passes for "honest" pottery; if I see myself as graceful, the pots will reflect this image. . . . During that time, an unnoticed process had been taking place. I had begun to see small but undeniable truths about myself, and had begun to be interested in seeing them. . . . I had come to realize that the solidly entrenched attitude toward results—"success"—poisoned all my efforts. . . . I began to be more and more interested in what the craft was revealing to me of myself.[42]

Whereas doing pottery is clearly very meaningful for Carla Needleman, many psychologists would insist that the correct term is "reinforcing." Meaning is too abstract to them, whereas reinforcement is not abstract at all. I would like to disagree and make the point that the two terms are equally abstract. An interesting conversation was published a few years ago between senior editor of *Psychology Today,* Kenneth Goodall, and Montrose Wolf, a pioneer researcher in behavior modification techniques. The conversation included the following exchange, that illustrates my point.

> WOLF: The thing that makes reinforcement less abstract is that you can see it and you—
>
> GOODALL: But you cannot see reinforcement.
>
> WOLF: You can see the data. You can shape a child's behavior, a social isolate for instance, by giving him praise so that his contacts with other children increase. You can then withdraw the praise—the reinforcer—and the isolate behavior will return. What you see there is reinforcement.
>
> GOODALL: Well, you see a behavior that you presume is reinforced. It is the behavior that you see.[43]

The investigator sees behavior and presumes that something is reinforcing. But why is it reinforcing? Because it is meaningful. That is no more abstract, it seems to me, than to just say it is reinforcing.

Experience

It has been said that meaning is to experience what measurement is to behavior.[44] It is true, however, that a phenomenological description is formulated from the co-investigator's verbal and nonverbal behavior. But the importance of the behavior is that it represents the co-investigator's underlying experience. The problem is that the behavior can in varying degrees represent or misrepresent the experience—what the co-investigator really means. So the job of phenomenological psychology is to devise methods to facilitate the accurate representation, by self-report behavior, of the components of a person's lived experience. These are generally referred to as "phenomenal worlds" and "intentionality."

Phenomenal Worlds

A phenomenal world is the reflective organization, the rationality, the individualized thoughts that a person refers to as reality—or at least reality as the individual sees it. This is "consciousness," which is often spoken of as the object of the phenomenologist's study.

Intentionality

The *pre*reflective, *non*rational, feeling-oriented part of experience can be called intentionality. This is the preverbal tending toward or orienting toward something that we usually, at some point, try to formulate into words. By putting it into words, it becomes part of our conscious awareness, or our phenomenal world. Specifically, intentionality is our spontaneous, bodily felt involvement in a situation before we have words for it. For example, one may break out into a cold sweat while talking with another person, without any conscious awareness of why. Or, one may be prayerful without uttering words.

Intentionality is in the realm of the unconscious which, along with conscious awareness, comprises the totality of human experience. Intentionality, as an integral part of experience, can play a significant role in the understanding a person has of a particular experience as well as in the communication of the meaning of that experience to someone else. Thus, the apostle Paul was able to experience (and I am sure that he communicated to others through his actions) the love of Christ, as well as the peace of God, with a depth that surpassed mental understanding only. (Eph. 3:19; Phil. 4:7).

Structure

Phenomenal worlds and intentionality are generally thought to merge into meaningful patterns of organization that we call structures of experience. We say, when doing a phenomenological study, that we are looking for the structure of an experience.

Perhaps the easiest way for the investigator to begin to identify the structure of a co-investigator's experience is to look for the expression of thoughts and feelings, both verbally and nonverbally. In the process the personal, spatial, and temporal aspects of the experience can begin to unfold.[45] In other words, how the co-investigator feels about him- or herself while in the situation being described, what the physical characteristics of the situation are, and how time is experienced in the situation—all begin to weave themselves into the fabric of the entire experience. Each one, of course, can be elaborated, depending on what seems to be most vital to the co-investigator. The co-investigator's experience of time, for instance, may be pursued because of his or her expression that it is experienced in terms of expansion ("I've never spent such a long twenty minutes in my life") or compression ("Time flies when you're havin' fun") or even suspension ("When I am with her I lose all sense of time").

In addition, a number of experiential details can further enrich the co-investigator's story, and they need to be noted by the investigator. These include orienting details of the experience (such as its clarity, intensity, or texture), details that shift back and forth between two poles (like faith and fear or love and hate), and details that undergird the entire experience (as in "the bottom line," or "the fertile ground" out of which the entire experience grows).[46] An example would be Psalm 18:1—"Fervently do I love Thee, O Lord, my strength" (Berkeley). "Fervently" would be an orienting experiential detail, "love" a shifting experiential detail, and "strength" the undergirding experiential detail. A good exercise would be to locate the experiential details in Carla Needleman's description of working at the craft of pottery.

Existential Validation

This is the name for the process of understanding between the investigator and co-investigator that verifies the meaning of the latter's experience. It is the human science counterpart to the statistical validation techniques used in the natural sciences. Some sort of validation is necessary to prevent solipsism, or basing one's belief that something is true entirely on the fact that it was personally experienced. Although existential validation is not a statistical procedure, this does not necessarily mean that it is any less powerful. Neither way is perfect, and both are statements of probability—the difference is that one is expressed in numbers, and the other is not. And both are ultimately commitments of faith; that makes them even.

Because the co-investigator's experience must be conceptualized, or put into words, and can be described in a variety of personally meaningful ways, phenomenological research is highly symbolic in nature. The unit of analysis is language or words, which are symbols. In natural science, a symbol is "operationally defined," or assumed for the purpose of the study to mean just one thing. It is referred to as a sign when it is thereby in a one-to-one relationship with reality. A symbol, on the other hand, has a one-to-many relationship with reality and is not defined or restricted in its meaning ahead of time.

The word that symbolizes the entire experience is what needs to be existentially validated. For example, in a phenomenological study of the experience of anxiety, the co-investigator's experience of anxiety, as described to the investigator, needs to be shown to be valid.

A symbol must meet five criteria to be existentially valid (I will use the symbol "love" as an example):

1. It is discovered, not invented. The experience is more original than conforming to a prior assumption. Love between two Christians is not the same as *the* experience of Christian love (the assumption that all Christian experiences of love are the same).
2. It points beyond itself. Love does not point to itself (which would be like being in love with being in love) but to the beloved.
3. It participates in that to which it points. It is actually a part of the total experience, as revealed by the nonverbal as well as verbal reactions to the beloved.
4. It changes. Love grows deeper over time.
5. It grows experientially. Love does not grow logically, through intellectual categories.[47]

Because existential validation concerns lived experience, the co-investigator as well as the symbol should change and grow. The primary characteristic of the co-investigator, for the experience to be existentially valid, then, is transformation.[48] There must be a definite change in the quality of the person's existence.

The remaining ingredient of the existential validation process is the communication of the meaning of the co-investigator's experience to the investigator, so that it is understood similarly by them both. As someone has said, it takes two to discover truth; one to speak it and one to understand it. Phenomenological research methodologies prescribe the steps for how this communication process should unfold.

Phenomenological Psychology: The Methods

Phenomenological inquiry begins in silence, with a call for "the spirit of generosity rather than for that of economy, for reverence rather than for subjugation, for the lens rather than for the hammer."[49]

There are several ways to proceed from such a humble beginning. There is no one way to do a phenomenological study, but there are many commonalities across the various research methods. I have tried to bring most of them together into the following:

Step One

The *approach* phase—a self-examination of presuppositions (beliefs, attitudes, hunches, and hypotheses) about the topic to be investigated and the investigation itself.

1. I can examine my approach by asking:
   a. Why am *I* involved with *this* topic *now*?
   b. How might my personality determine my selection of this particular topic?
   c. How might certain demand characteristics in my life affect my reason for doing this study and for doing it in this way?
2. There are no preestablished criteria for deciding when to terminate this or any of the other phases of the investigation. Termination of a phase of the research is appropriate, however, when there is a sense, an empty but distinct feel-

ing, of being satisfied that what has been done is adequate in the face of the tension of its not being absolutely complete or final.

Step Two

The *question* phase—formulating the initial interview question. The success of this question depends on the extent to which it taps the co-investigator's sense of the phenomenon as lived experience rather than mere theoretical knowledge.

Example:

"Try to remember the last time you were (anxious). Describe what you did and how you felt."

Step Three

The *selection* phase—selecting a co-investigator. Experience with the topic to be investigated and ability to relate and express oneself generally suffice as selection criteria.

Step Four

The *collection* phase—collecting the co-investigator's descriptive responses. This is done in one-on-one dialogue, with the emphasis being on present experiencing of the phenomenon under investigation and its effects. A dialogue begins with the initial interview question and ends upon agreement of the investigator and co-investigator. During the interview, other preformulated questions may or may not be used, and a tape recorder is usually used to make the interview data available for analysis later.

Step Five

The *analysis* phase—analyzing the data.

1. Read all the descriptive responses as transcribed from the tape.
2. Re-read the responses and note the most significant phrases. Repetitions should be combined.
3. Organize the significant phrases into related clusters or themes.

4. Refer the themes back to the original responses. Ask whether there is anything contained in the responses that is not accounted for in the themes, and whether the themes propose anything not implied in the original responses.
5. Synthesize the themes into a summary description.
6. Return to the co-investigator and dialogue about the adequacy of the summary description compared with his or her actual lived experience. Work all clarifications and modifications into the final product. Relevant information from each of the six phases (approach, question, selection, collection, analysis, validation) of the research should be included in the report of the research.

Step Six

The *validation* phase—validating the summary description. Steps 1 through 5 satisfy the communication criterion for the existential validation of the experience. The final step is to check the summary description against the remaining existential validation criteria. Was the experience discovered (not invented), did it point beyond itself, did it participate in that to which it pointed, did it change, and did it grow experientially? And, did the experience transform the co-investigator?[50]

Representative studies in the literature would include Adrian van Kaam's study of the experience of really feeling understood,[51] Emily Stevick's investigation of the experience of anger,[52] Ernest Keen's study of a five-year-old changing her mind,[53] and Paul Colaizzi's research into the process of existential change occasioned by reading.[54] Although these four studies adequately portray the diversity of methods within phenomenological psychology, all but the Colaizzi study are significantly less than ideal in fully incorporating dialogue into its methodology.

I have found the Stevick study to be the most interesting example of phenomenological research. The section of her chapter where she records part of an investigator-co-investigator dialogue reads like a therapy session. Probably the most sophisticated example of phenomenological research is the Colaizzi study. And finally, I would say that Christopher Stones has provided us with the best example of a phenomenological method with several applications.[55]

Conclusion

We come finally to the question of how these recommended changes would enhance the quality of integration. I have shown previously that changing psychology *can* help integration. Now the question is *how*.

The answer to the question involves the fact that as Christians we want God to permeate everything we do. In other words, integration involves God's activity in varying degrees as we discover his truths through the various disciplines and bring them together in a coherent fashion, and we therefore want to maximize the degree of such involvement in both the discovery phase and the bringing together phase. In order to accomplish this, we will need to make some basic changes in psychology to allow space for more of the activity of God in the research process.

Again, the question is *how*. First, I would like to point out that the recommended changes allow for the activity of God in more than the foundational presuppositions upon which psychology rests and the ethical application of the findings in which research in psychology results, which exceeds the emphasis of most other Christian psychologists. The recommended changes provide the opportunity for God to be more directly involved in the middle of the psychological research process, as well as at both ends. God's activity is acknowledged and used in the conduct of the research itself (collecting and analyzing data) as well as in the preresearch selection of a methodology and the postresearch use of the results.[56]

Human-science oriented methodologies open the door for God's direct activity in the conduct of a study by allowing his truths to be revealed through lived experience. They are not forced to wind their way through laboratory approximations or deceptive manipulations. Rather, God can speak more directly through real-life dialogue between two people trying to help each other get to the truth of the matter. This is how I see the recommended changes helping our integrative efforts. And I believe a psychology that is an intentional channel for God's revelation will help much more than one that is only neutral, the latter being the case for those psychologists who neglect the activity of God in the middle of the research process.[57]

One final note is important for a balanced perspective. Psychology as a human science is not the *only* answer, nor is phenomenological psychology necessarily the *best* answer. Natural science-oriented methods are totally appropriate when dealing with certain kinds of questions, and human-science methods with other kinds of questions. British brain physiologist Donald MacKay said it well.

> The scientist professionally has one great aim—to know more and understand more of our mysterious world from a detached spectator's standpoint. But he has to recognize also that there are many aspects of reality which can be known only through becoming involved with them, so that in order to have knowledge of these he is obliged, by his own ruling principle of "openness to evidence", to give up scientific detachment.[58]

It is important that we have alternative methods and that we let the question dictate the method, not the other way around. In addition, although I have picked phenomenological psychology as the best representative of the human-science orientation, I do not believe it is the only one or that it cannot and will not be improved upon. Our investment should not be primarily in phenomenological psychology as such, but rather, first and foremost in knowing God's truth by whatever means possible.

Notes

1. Collins, G. R. *The rebuilding of psychology: An integration of psychology and Christianity.* Wheaton: Tyndale House, 1977.
2. Koteskey, R. L. *Psychology from a Christian perspective*. Nashville: Abingdon, 1980, chap. 11.

3. Van Leeuwen, M. S. *The sorcerer's apprentice: A Christian look at the changing face of psychology*. Downers Grove, Ill.: Inter-Varsity, 1982, preface, chap. 3.

4. Mixter, R. L. ed., *Evolution and Christian thought today,* 2d ed. Grand Rapids: Wm. B. Eerdmans, 1960; Henry, C. F. H. ed., *Horizons of science: Christian scholars speak out*. New York: Harper & Row, 1978.

5. Kulik, J. A.; Brown, D. R.; Vestewig, R. E.; and Wright, J. *Undergraduate education in psychology*. Washington, D. C.: American Psychological Association, 1973, p. 39.

6. Van Leeuwen, *Sorcerer's apprentice,* p. 119.

7. See A. H. Maslow, *The psychology of science: A reconnaissance*. Chicago: Henry Regnery, 1966, pp. 112–14.

8. Rubin, Z. Taking deception for granted. *Psychology Today* 17(3) (1983), p. 74.

9. Ibid., p. 75.

10. Adair, J. G. *The human subject: The social psychology of the psychological experiment*. Boston: Little, Brown, 1973; Miller, A. G. ed., *The social psychology of psychological research*. New York: The Free Press, 1972.

11. Bassett, R. L.; Basinger, D.; and Livermore, P. Lying in the laboratory: Deception in human research from psychological, philosophical, and theological perspectives. *Journal of the American Scientific Affiliation* 34 (1982): 201–12.

12. Bakan, D. *On method: Toward a reconstruction of psychological investigation*. San Francisco: Jossey-Bass, 1967, chap. 4.

13. McGuire, W. J. The yin and yang of progress in social psychology: Seven Koan. *Journal of Personality and Social Psychology* 26 (1973), p. 449.

14. See H. L. Dreyfus, *What computers can't do: A critique of artificial reason.* New York: Harper & Row, 1972; Lewis, J., and Towers, B. *Naked ape or homo sapiens?* New York: New American Library, 1973.

15. Sanford, N. *Issues in personality theory.* San Francisco: Jossey-Bass, 1970, preface.

16. Campbell, D. T. On the conflicts between biological and social evolution and between psychology and moral tradition. *American Psychologist* 30 (1975): 1103–26.

17. Argyris, C. Some unintended consequences of rigorous research. *Psychological Bulletin* 70 (1968), p. 185.

18. Ibid., p. 186.

19. Kaplan, A. *The conduct of inquiry: Methodology for behavioral science*. San Francisco: Chandler, 1964, pp. 28–29.

20. Bakan, *On method,* pp. 44–45.

21. Harris, T. G. Jung and old: An introduction. *Psychology Today* 5(7) (1971): 43.

22. See L. Berkowitz, Simple views of aggression: An essay review. *American Scientist* 57 (1969): 372–83.

23. Harlow, H. F.; Harlow, M. K.; and Suomi, S. J. From thought to therapy: Lessons from a primate laboratory. *American Scientist* 59 (1971), p. 545–6.

24. May, R. *Psychology and the human dilemma*. Princeton, N.J.: Van Nostrand, 1967, pp. 3–4.

25. Van Leeuwen, *Sorcerer's apprentice,* quotations on pp. 77, 81, 91.

26. Ibid., pp. 36, 116, 117.

27. Goleman, D. A conversation with Ulric Neisser. *Psychology Today* 17(5) (1983), p. 62.

28. MacLeod, R. B. *The persistent problems of psychology*. Pittsburgh: Duquesne University, 1975. See especially the introduction, pp. 1–16.

29. See E. P. Willems, and H. L. Raush, eds., *Naturalistic viewpoints in psychological research*. New York: Holt, Rinehart and Winston, 1969.

30. See S. J. Gould, *The mismeasure of man*. New York: W. W. Norton, 1981.

31. Bakan, *On method,* chap. 1.

32. Rosenthal, R. *Experimenter effects in behavioral research*. New York: Appleton-Century-Crofts, 1966.

33. Weber, S. J., and Cook, T. D. Subject effects in laboratory research: An examination of subject roles, demand characteristics, and valid inference. *Psychological Bulletin* 77 (1972): 273–95.

34. Gergen, K. J. Social psychology as history. *Journal of Personality and Social Psychology* 26 (1973): 309–20.

35. Orne, M. T. Hypnosis, motivation, and the ecological validity of the psychological experiment. In *Nebraska symposium on motivation 1970,* eds., W. J. Arnold and M. M. Page. Lincoln: University of Nebraska, 1971, pp. 187–265.

36. See H. Spiegelberg, *The phenomenological movement: A historical introduction,* 2d ed. The Hague, Netherlands: Martinus Nijhoff, 1969, vol. 2, chap. 14.

37. Misiak, H., and Sexton, V. S. *Phenomenological, existential, and humanistic psychologies: A historical survey*. New York: Grune & Stratton, 1973; Spiegelberg, H. *Phenomenology in psychology and psychiatry: A historical introduction*. Evanston, Ill.: Northwestern University, 1972.

38. Snygg, D., and Combs, A. W. *Individual behavior: A new frame of reference for psychology*. New York: Harper & Row, 1949; Wann, T. W. ed., *Behaviorism and phenomenology: Contrasting bases for modern psychology*. Chicago: University of Chicago, 1964.

39. Giorgi, A.; Fischer, W. F.; and Von Eckartsberg, R. eds., *Duquesne studies in phenomenological psychology,* vol. 1. Pittsburgh: Duquesne University, 1971; Giorgi, A.; Fischer, C. T.; and Murray, E. L. eds., *Duquesne studies in phenomenological psychology,* vol. 2. Pittsburgh: Duquesne University, 1975; Giorgi, A.; Knowles, R.; and Smith, D. L. eds., *Duquesne studies in phenomenological psychology,* vol. 3. Pittsburgh: Duquesne University, 1979; Giorgi, A.; Barton, A.; and Maes, C. eds, *Duquesne studies in phenomenological psychology,* vol. 4. Pittsburgh: Duquesne University, 1983; Giorgi, A. *Psychology as a human science: A phenomenologically based approach*. New York: Harper & Row, 1970.

40. Merleau-Ponty, M. What is phenomenology? trans. Colin Smith. In *Phenomenology of religion: Eight modern descriptions of the essence of religion,* ed., J. D. Bettis. New York: Harper & Row, 1969, pp. 13–30; Giorgi, A. Phenomenology and the foundations of psychology. In *Nebraska symposium on motivation 1975,* ed., J. K. Cole and W. J. Arnold, Lincoln: University of Nebraska, 1976, pp. 281–348.

41. Lewis, C. S. *The abolition of man*. New York: Macmillan, 1947, p. 91.

42. Needleman, C. Potter's progress: Self-understanding and the lessons of craft. *Psychology Today* 13(1) (1979): 78–86.

43. Goodall, K. "This little girl won't interact with the other little girls, and she crawls around a lot": A conversation about behavior modification with Montrose M. Wolf. *Psychology Today* 7(1) (1973), p. 66.

44. Giorgi, A. The experience of the subject as a source of data in a psychological experiment. In *Duquesne studies,* vol. 1, chap. 4.

45. For similar ideas, see R. B. MacLeod, Psychological phenomenology: A propaedeutic to a scientific psychology. In *Toward unification in psychology,* ed., J. R. Royce. Toronto: University of Toronto, 1970, chap. 6.

46. Ibid, pp. 253–60.
47. Taken, in modified form, from J. R. Royce, ed., *Psychology and the symbol: An interdisciplinary symposium*. New York: Random House, 1965, pp. 19–21.
48. Ibid, p. 21.
49. Spiegelberg, *Phenomenological movement,* p. 657.
50. See especially P. F. Colaizzi, Psychological research as the phenomenologist views it. In *Existential-phenomenological alternatives for psychology,* eds., R. S. Valle and M. King. New York: Oxford University, 1978, chap. 3.
51. van Kaam, A. *Existential foundations of psychology*. Pittsburgh: Duquesne University, 1966, chap. 10.
52. Stevick, E. L. An empirical investigation of the experience of anger. In *Duquesne studies,* vol. 1, chap. 10.
53. Keen, E. *A primer in phenomenological psychology*. New York: Holt, Rinehart and Winston, 1975, chap. 1.
54. Colaizzi, Psychological research.
55. Stones, C. R. Research: Toward a phenomenological praxis. In *An introduction to phenomenological psychology,* ed., D. Kruger. Pittsburgh: Duquesne University, 1981 chap. 4.
56. Farnsworth, K. E. *Integrating psychology and theology: Elbows together but hearts apart.* Washington, D. C.: University Press of America, 1981, preface, chap. 2.
57. See M. J. DeVries. Beyond integration: New directions. *The CAPS Bulletin* 7(3) (1981): 1–5.
58. MacKay, D. M. *The clockwork image: A Christian perspective on science*. Downers Grove, Ill.: Inter-Varsity, 1974, p. 38.

2

Theology

Change is also in the air in theology. There is a fairly consistent pattern to the questions being asked about "doing theology" and about theologians themselves.

> What is theology, who does it, and how should it be done?[1]
>
> Who does theology, where is it done, and what should the focus be?[2]
>
> Who are the theologians, what do they believe, and where are they changing?[3]

Answers to these questions have obvious implications. First, the extent to which they would positively affect the quality of theological research is the same extent to which they would improve the overall quality of the integration process. This means that theological research and psychological research together comprise the methodological starting point referred to in chapter 1.

Another implication is that theology and theologians need to change. And with all those questions, there are many places for change in many different directions. There is no way to entertain all the possibilities here, nor am I qualified to do so; however, I would like to deal with three areas that are significant from an integrative perspective.

First is the question of *who* should be doing theology. Should theology continue, as in the past, to be predominantly a white, male, Euro-American enterprise? Second is the question of *how* theology is being done. Is biblical research strictly the accumulation of facts perceived by "immaculate perception" through the rational application of hermeneutical (interpretive) procedures? Can it be assumed to be uncontaminated by human factors? Third is the question of *focus*. Would it not be valuable to study religious experience more directly than has been done in the past, and in so doing emphasizing participant observation rather than detached observation?

These questions provide the backdrop for an important issue that confronts us here: Since theological methods can be called into question just as readily as psychological methods, should not theological methods be examined before facts that they produce are integrated? Equally important, would improvements in the methods open some new doors for communicating with God?

Who Should Do Theology?

> In the past, theology has usually been done by the "experts," who, although they sometimes worked in the heat of the battle, more often worked in the relative calm and detachment of the seminary or university or monastery, using texts of the past as their basic resources, producing large and scholarly tomes of "systematic theology," replete with footnotes, foreign phrases, and intricate arguments that could conserve and interpret the past for the sake of the present. The orientation was in large measure to books, ideas, concepts, and modes of argument, rather than to human struggle, anguish, pain, and exploitation. A finished position was being sought, a restatement of "the faith once delivered to the saints," that, if not destined to be definitive forever, might at least be normative for a long time to come.
>
> There is no point in trying to demean or put down the need for

> such discursive, rational, and somewhat abstract endeavor. There is, however, a point in suggesting that no matter how valuable such activity has been in the past, and might once again be in the future, it is not the crying need of the present.[4]

Theology is seen by well-known theologian Robert McAfee Brown as too much the province of experts, who are detached and sheltered from firsthand participation in the basic human struggles that take up the daily life of the majority of the human race. Harvard theologian Harvey Cox refers to these experts' theology as a theology of the elite.

> The minimal conditions . . . for doing theology . . . include the ability to read and write in at least one language, some familiarity with the received tradition of concepts and categories, sufficient leisure to think, and the power to get one's ideas published or otherwise heard. But these conditions are available only to people who have benefited from privileged educational opportunities and whose present position in life frees them from a daily struggle against hunger and cold. These minimal "class" conditions exclude the vast majority of people from ever being considered theologians, at least in this respect.
>
> I am not interested in scolding. Theology has always been produced by an elite, and although the voices of blacks, feminists and other previously excluded groups have undercut some established perspectives, they have not done much to challenge the class bias. What I am asking is whether the conditions that automatically exclude all but middle-class people from doing theology make a significant difference *in the theology itself*. . . . Or is it something one can safely ignore?[5]

These two rather lengthy statements issue a strong challenge to theology of the experts and the elite. A broader perspective is needed, one that includes representative views from all of God's children. That is the crying need that we cannot safely ignore.

The Liberation of Theology

If we are going to liberate theology from the narrow confines of the past, we will need some guidelines. Robert McAfee Brown recommends the following:

1. Theology should be an open-ended process. For the present, at least, we need to be willing to rethink some of our past theological conclusions in light of Christian perspectives other than our own.

2. Theology should be a corporate process. We do not need some individual, some star, to appear on the horizon with an all-new set of theological propositions. Rather, we need the cooperation of Christians from all walks of life and geographic locations to work together to establish an ongoing corporate theological process for the discernment of God's truths.

3. Theology should be a self-correcting process. We need to recognize that widespread representation in the theological process of Christians from different classes, backgrounds, and sexes will create a diversity of opinions as to what the Bible says. These differences need to be prayerfully considered so that each view can point out the mote in another's theological eye and in turn be helped to see the beam in its own.

4. Theology should be an engaged process. That is, those who do theology must do in their lives what they think in their minds. Theological thinking must be engaged thinking—doing, not just cogitating.[6]

I would add to these a fifth guideline, offered by South American theologian René Padilla:

5. Theology should be a process of "hermeneutical circulation."[7] Theology must be, in other words, a process of continuous reciprocal interaction between Scripture and the historical context of the theologian. Thus, a better understanding of Scripture leads to a greater understanding of historical context, and a deeper understanding of the context leads to richer comprehension of the truths in Scripture.

Brown's emphasis on process and Padilla's emphasis on context are probably the primary factors in the quest for a liberated theology. The problem, as Padilla sees it, is that theology in Europe and North America has been largely an academic exercise.[8] It has assumed that knowledge of truth is possible separate from the practice of truth. This is the intellectualization of truth and the rationalistic framework from which Padilla believes theology must be liberated. Guidelines that emphasize an open-ended, corporate, self-correcting, engaged theological process and the lived context of the theologian should go far in accomplishing that task. By their very nature, the guidelines should also provide theology with its much-needed broadened perspective.

Liberating Theologies

When theology is liberated, then theology becomes liberating.[9] This is easily seen in the theological reflections of Blacks, feminists, Asians, Native Americans, and Hispanics that have recently been brought together into a single volume.[10] The value of such diverse liberating theologies, for integration, is that lives get changed, and changed lives produce new perspectives. Each grouping of Christians has its own historical context, and when that is affirmed and made part of the theological process (through hermeneutical circulation), the particular perspective that results is bound to bring to light certain aspects of truth that Christians operating within other cultural contexts might not have seen.

For example, black theology has given me a much deeper understanding of the biblical sense of hope—based solely on reliance on God's provision—as opposed to the more superficial sense of optimism and wishful thinking that permeates so many of our white churches today. And biblical feminism has given me a much greater understanding of the female as well as male qualities of God and deeper appreciation for biblical characters—great women of God—like Abigail, and Phoebe, and Lydia, that I had never heard about in years of listening to male preachers.

I do not expect the result to be new truths, necessarily, that have been missed through all the past years of theologizing, but certainly different angles on the same truths that we have known all along. Such expanded understanding greatly enhances the possibilities for integration. It brings into view a more varied and richer expression of theological truths to be integrated with their psychological counterparts.

Biblical Feminism

Of all the different liberating theologies, the one that has affected me most personally is biblical feminism. At one level—the intellectual—I have become thoroughly convinced of the dire need for women biblical scholars. There have been excellent arguments through the years for women being directly involved in the exegesis (critical interpretation) of Scripture, including participation in the translation process for new editions of the Bible. One of the most compelling of these was made over half a century ago by medical doctor and biblical scholar Katherine Bushnell. Her words call out to us through the years and demand a hearing.

> The printed Word tells you half the story, and your heart's experience the other half. . . . The world, the Church and women are suffering sadly from woman's lack of ability to read the Word of God in its original languages. There are truths therein that speak to the deepest needs of a woman's heart, and that give light upon problems that women alone are called upon to solve. Without knowledge of the original, on the part of a sufficient number of women to influence the translation of the Bible in accordance with their perception of the meaning of these truths, these needed passages will remain uninterpreted, or misinterpreted. . . . We must remember that no translation can rise much above the character of the translator. . . . He cannot properly render what has not as yet entered in the least into his own consciousness as the truth.[11]

For example:

> The interpretation of Gen. 3:16 has had a history something like this: Men of old found a phrase here that seemed to have to do with woman's relation to her husband, but it was beyond their comprehension. Unconsciously these men of olden time have consulted their own ideas of what a wife *should be,* in her relation to her husband, and inserted those ideas into their interpretation. The interpretation has been accepted by other men, without challenge, because it conformed to their unsanctified wishes, and handed on from generation to generation, until it became weighty through "tradition". . . . Prejudice blinds men, even in their treatment of the

> Word of God, if a faulty rendering coincides with their preconceptions.[12]

Psychologically, I believe she is right. It can be difficult, if not impossible, to perceive something that you cannot conceive of as a possibility.

I have also been personally and deeply affected by biblical feminism at the emotional level. Whereas translation work is one area of biblical scholarship, teaching is another, and it is in the latter area that I have become emotionally involved. I have seen one God-fearing woman after another, whose only agenda is single-minded obedience to Jesus Christ in the furthering of his kingdom, excluded from the teaching ministry of the church—except for reading Bible stories to little children. I exaggerate because I want to make a point: women are excluded by definition. Not by deed, but by definition. They are not men. No matter that a woman has a thorough knowledge of Scripture and consistently applies it in her daily life. No matter that others, men and women alike, would be richly blessed by her teaching. She is not a man.

This all came crashing in on me a few years ago, after we had made a major move. There were many unexpected costs, and we were brought to utter dependence on the Lord for our provision. This was because we chose not to change our giving habits to favor ourselves for a while to give us time to recover. No, we continued as always to give right off the top—at the first of each month—to the Lord's work. How could we stop giving to those who were as bad off as we were, or even worse?

There were times when we literally did not know where the next meal would come from, and because of that we learned the true meaning of sacrificial giving, and of God's provision. As the weeks became months, God showed my wife verse after verse in the Bible that clarified his plan for us: plant, expect a harvest, and give thanks. As we lived out these principles, and no one went hungry, it then seemed only natural to give public testimony to the Lord's provision in our lives.

The church we were attending at the time, however, did not permit women to teach men, so the forum my wife was given for sharing those principles was one of the women's study groups. The principal forum in that church, as in most churches, was the Sunday morning service—that was where the most important learning was to take place. Yet Sunday after Sunday the men who spoke did not seem to be very well grounded in Scripture, nor were they able to give evidence that their abstract ideas could make a difference in anyone's life. In short, they could not teach.

Then one Sunday a young man stood in the pulpit and said, "As I was thinking last night about what I could say today, nothing came to me, so I thought about this book I've been reading." My wife and I just sat there fighting back tears. Here was one part of the body trying to fake it, while another part—with a clear message from God and a capable teacher at all age levels—had to stifle herself—and the Holy Spirit.

Biblical feminism has shown me at all levels of my being that we need to have women as well as men interpreting and teaching the truths of Scripture. We need women doing theology too.

Biblical Hermeneutics

Focusing on women in the discussion of who should be doing theology creates a natural bridge to the question of how it is being done. This is the question that deals with the method. It is the hermeneutical question.

Christian philosopher Nicholas Wolterstorff likens the method used by many Christians in discerning biblical truths regarding women to a cafeteria-like interpretive approach. The approach has two strategies: "pick-and-choose" and the "selectively-applied-principle" strategy.[13] In other words, take what you like and ignore what you do not like, and extract a general principle from a particular text but then apply it only where you want to. An example of the latter is concluding from the "husband of one wife" section of 1 Timothy 3 that women cannot meet that qualification and therefore cannot hold church office. But why, asks Wolterstorff, do the people who arrive at that conclusion not also agitate to keep unmarried and widowed *men* out of church office?

An example of the pick-and-choose strategy is to interpret 1 Timothy 2:8–15 as saying that women cannot have authority over men in the church, and then ignore the injunctions to raise hands while praying and dress modestly, without jewelry. Wolterstorff rightly points out that to say some injunctions are culturally conditioned but some are not is clearly wrong in this case, because Paul makes no such distinction.

There probably are several other interpretive strategies that could be brought out into the light of day. The point is, however, that as much as we would like to, we cannot assume that our interpretations are perfect replicas of the original. Nor can we even assume that the process of interpretation is an entirely logical, rational undertaking. Human factors do get in the way. Let us take a look at two of them, the world view factor and the nonrationality factor.

The World View Factor

Christian historian Mark Noll maintains that the interpretation of Scripture has been deeply influenced by the changing tides of scientific ways of thinking ever since the days of Francis Bacon. Noll documents the development of the particular influence of Bacon, Isaac Newton, and the Scottish realists, and their impact on the theological methods of the time. The chief characteristics of Baconian science (the overall name for the entire development) are emphases on induction (reasoning from particular ideas to general laws) and observation by experiment. Reliable knowledge, according to Baconian science, "arises from the accumulation of perceived facts apprehended directly by objective observers."[14]

Noll further maintains that twentieth-century evangelicals find the Baconian world view the most satisfactory of all scientific world views. That being the case, he wonders about the hermeneutical consequences.

> Why do evangelicals read the Bible as we do? Is it not at least possible that it is Baconianism, rather than a principle of Scripture itself, that has encouraged some evangelicals to regard the Bible as a compendium of separate facts and commands rather than as a unified revelation of the character and acts of God? Discussions over the ordination of women sometimes illustrate this tendency. In addressing this issue, are we not prone to hurling individual texts at one another (Gal. 3:28; I Tim. 2:12), instead of examining the general character of God's dealing with his people from Genesis through Revelation?[15]

It certainly is possible that one's scientific world view will directly affect one's approach to Scripture. It is also possible that a world view of an entirely different sort—male chauvinism—can affect one's hermeneutics.

Christian educators Berkeley and Alvera Mickelsen definitely believe that a chauvinistic world view has hurt our Bible translations.

> We doubt if any of the men on translation committees or who did their own translations are conscious of any male chauvinism. All are honest, godly scholars, dedicated to doing their best work, trying faithfully to bring to today's readers the message of the Bible.
>
> But like all of us, these translators grew up in a society that assumed males should dominate home, church, and society at large. It has been as much a part of our culture (and of most pagan cultures) as the air we breathe. Translators naturally tend to read and interpret the Bible from the framework in which they have lived and thought.[16]

As a statement of support, the editor of *Christianity Today*, where the Mickelsen's article appeared, added the following footnote:

> The Mickelsens have made no attempt to be exhaustive in pointing out examples of chauvinistic translations. The King James Version has twisted many a passage to save the male ego—or its chauvinistic theology.
>
> The King James Version, for example, reverses the Greek order

> to place Aquilla before Priscilla in deference to the husband—in spite of the fact that in the biblical text, Priscilla is clearly the leader (Acts 18:26). In I Timothy 2:11, the King James Version translates *hesychia* "Let the woman learn in silence," but when referring to men (II Thess. 3:16), it renders the same word, "with quietness they work and eat." Psalm 68:11 reads, "great was the company of those that publish the word of the Lord" in spite of the fact that the Hebrew is explicitly feminine: "great was the company of those women who publish the word of the Lord." On the other hand, the KJV correctly notes the feminine Junia in Romans 16:7 in contrast with most contemporary translations that with little or no justification transform *mir abile dictu,* the woman Junia, into the man Junias to avoid the unthinkable—a woman among the apostles![17]

Whether world views are unconscious cultural by-products or consciously motivated tools of the ego, they obviously can affect the interpretive process. Closely associated with the unconscious use of world views is the human factor of nonrationality.

The Nonrationality Factor

First, what does "nonrational" mean? I am using the term synonymously with "intentionality," as defined earlier. It refers to the prereflective, feeling-oriented part of experience. It is in the realm of the unconscious, a preverbal tending toward or orienting toward something. Thus, we can liken it to unconscious motivation.

Christian psychologist Cedric Johnson in a recent book explores some psychological factors that are involved in biblical interpretation, including unconscious motivation.[18] One of the more interesting unconscious processes he mentions is transference, or relating to an authority as a reflection of an earlier conflict. Since the Bible is authoritative, it is very possible for a person to transfer to it a negative response to authority from the past. Johnson points out, for example, the possibility of a Christian woman who was rejected by her father as she grew up transferring her fear of authority to Scripture. Her unconscious reaction could be rebellion against the Bible as too judgmental, which could significantly affect her method of interpretation.

In a previous publication, I have argued for the importance of understanding the role of the nonrational in the biblical content itself. My coauthors and I illustrated our point by exegeting two verses, one from each of the two testaments of the Bible. We concluded that 1 Thessalonians 5:17 intends "pray without ceasing" to mean a nonrational, "prayerful attitude of silent expectancy that makes possible the uninterrupted continuance of prayer between times of verbal, or spoken prayer," as well as verbal prayer itself.[19] Similarly, we concluded that in Jeremiah 9:24 there is a distinction between "understanding" and "knowing," so that the former is intellectual (rational), while the latter is emotional (nonrational) as well as intellectual. In the context of the surrounding verses, then, Jeremiah is using "understanding" and "knowing" together to suggest an intimacy that would not be possible without the nonrational component.

Rationalistic Bias

Although the reality of the nonrational in the method and in the content is obvious to me, there are those who would disagree. The disagreement takes the form of a rationalistic bias against anything that is not expressed verbally and arrived at through reason. In other words, feelings are categorically distrusted. Content is always interpreted in rational categories, and method is considered to be an entirely rational process.

Because of rationalistic bias, it would be easy to miss the intimate nature of knowing intended by Jeremiah, or to fail to detect a fear of judgment in one's handling of Scripture. Yet,

> There seems to be widespread suspicion of any hermeneutic process which incorporates the idea that scriptural interpretation is in part prereflective, personalized perception. It is obvious to us, however, that scriptural interpretation is, by its very nature, a human activity albeit one that is guided by the Holy Spirit. And we believe that the Holy Spirit can work through one's feelings as well as one's thoughts, although not in either case perfectly all of the time because of human finiteness and fallenness. It is assumed by many in the evangelical subculture, however, that the truths in Scripture can be discovered only by presupposing that we know

> those truths through the use of an objective, impersonal methodology. To introduce the integrative notion of personal, nonrational perception intermingling with precise, rational methods of interpretation is heretical. In other words, if the nonrational is acknowledged as part of the hermeneutic process, and thus coterminous with rational hermeneutics, the precision of knowing God's propositional revelation is suddenly endangered by factors of an imprecise, subjective nature. This simply cannot be allowed, for fear of undermining the authority of Scripture.[20]

An overbearing assumption of methodological purity goes hand in hand with another characteristic of rationalistic bias, epistemological certainty. This is the belief that we can know with absolute certainty what the Bible says. And the corollary is that if there is any erosion in the methodological purity of our hermeneutics, then we can never know with certainty what the Bible says.[21] This is a confused and unnecessary conclusion.

We do not need a perfect method to satisfy our desire to know something with certainty. Given the nature of human knowing, we would not recognize a perfect method even if we had one. What we do have is our human imperfection and divine intervention. It is our firm conviction as Christians that our Lord can and does reveal his truths in spite of our impure methods. But because of our impure methods, we cannot claim to know those truths with absolute certainty. Even so, we trust that we can know with sufficient certainty the truths that God grants us to know. In addition, we confidently believe that since they are God's truths, they are absolutely true.

Christian philosopher Arthur Holmes uses the word "certitude" for the kind of confidence and conviction we are discussing. Whatever the word, my purpose is to shift the focus from the absoluteness of my certainty to the absoluteness of God's truth, from proof of the one to faith in the other. I do not think it is worthwhile, in other words, to try to *prove* that I am absolutely right about something. It is much more fruitful to try to *justify my faith* as absolutely true.[22]

We must compensate, then, for Baconism, male chauvinism, negative unconscious motivation, and rationalistic bias. Consider Cedric Johnson's conclusion:

> The perspective of the interpreter imparts both the distortion as well as the discovery of meaning. We also need to recognize that the Word of God has shaped whole cultures, altered nations, permeated legal and ethical systems, and changed lives. While our human preunderstanding acts as a lens through which we see the meaning of Scripture, the reverse is also true—meaning shapes our preunderstanding and the resultant theoretical, political, and cultural systems.[23]

A Christian world view can function as an interpretive framework to help us in the discovery and application of God's truths.[24] But as we mature, we do so in feeling as well as thought, which allows us to bring an increasingly greater capacity for discernment and personal application to the reading of Scripture. This provides a much deeper way for God to convict us with his truth and for us to commit ourselves to it than relying exclusively on a few intellectual presuppositions and not growing as a whole person. Spiritual growth involves our feelings as well as our intellectual preunderstandings, and whether they initially work for our benefit or harm, they both can and do change.[25] The Word of God progressively converts us at every level of our being.

Religious Experience

I want to affirm Scripture as the final authority in matters that are essential to faith and practice. I also believe, however, that God reveals some of his truths in other ways than through the written words of the Bible. One of those ways is through religious experiences.

What are religious experiences? Irish theologian Dermot Lane distinguishes among ordinary experience, depth experience, and religious experience.[26] Ordinary experiences are concerned with the everyday, tangible reality of objects and events. Depth experiences are those meaningful inner moments of appreciation of truth, beauty, and love. Religious experiences are moments of encounter with the immanent yet transcendent God who grounds all of reality.

Technically, reading the Bible is a religious experience, when its Author is encountered through its pages. Other religious experiences include auditory and visionary experiences, speaking in tongues, and such states of consciousness as the ecstatic trance. Often the context for such experiences is one of prayer, praise, meditation, or worship.

Thus, "every theology is an attempt to decode a religious experience."[27] "Theology, from beginning to end, is about the critical unpacking of the revelation of God that takes place in human experience through faith." It is "faith seeking understanding that is critically grounded in the experience of the revelation of God."[28] This is why, in answer to my earlier questions, we have no choice but to study religious experience itself as intently as we study biblical data. And, it is why we must accept conclusions arrived at from subjective religious experience. We must come to understand as clearly as possible the process that connects human subjectivity and divine objectivity—whether the object is the Bible or God himself—a process that is, simultaneously, both subjective and objective.

The Archetypal Understanding of Edwards and Otto

Undoubtedly, there are religious experiences that are nothing more than subjectivism resulting from a loss of contact with reality; but it is equally certain there are bona fide subjective religious experiences that arise out of contact with objective reality. Looking back in history for perspective, I am very much impressed with the life and work of the Puritan Jonathan Edwards. He was the one who struck the dominant chord for the place of subjectivity in human encounter with the Holy.

Edwards's view was a balanced one. He vigorously countered the scholastic psychology of his time (the eighteenth century), which separated the person into related but separate faculties, and the rationalistic bias of the surrounding culture that subordinated emotion to reason. Edwards could not accept the idea that "unruly affection" must be subordinated to "sober reason." Rather, he preferred to talk about reason that is passionate balanced with affection that is intellectual.[29]

Religious historian Richard Hutch understands Edwards's psychology in terms of "heat" and "light."

> On the one hand, there are the rationalists that maintain that religious experience is best understood in terms of "light," or cold reason. On the other hand, there are the enthusiasts who maintain that religious experience is best understood in terms of heat or fervent emotion. The one tends to lead toward dead formalism, and the other tends toward fanaticism and excess. Edwards was forever maintaining that both sides in themselves are wrong. Religious experience cannot be characterized in terms of one part of the human personality but as an integrated whole consisting of "a burning and shining light."[30]

The polar extremes of rationalist-light-reason-formalism and enthusiast-heat-emotion-fanaticism are still with us in the twentieth century, in spite of the integrative work of Jonathan Edwards. There are still those who see the only value in religious experience as the rational content. At the other extreme there are "charismaniacs" who value only the expression of fervent emotion.

An exception to such polarization is the work of Germany's Rudolf Otto, whose emphasis was very similar to Edwards's. The similarity begins to show up in his contrast between "darkness" and "light."

For Otto, unremitting light illumines the pettiness of life so that we must divert our attention to our own smallness and away from God's greatness. It illuminates our intellect so that we are able to hide God with our words while satisfying ourselves that we thereby have more of him. Continuous light deludes us into thinking that because we are able to name God, we can somehow possess him. Darkness, on the other hand, causes us to look up to God in awe and wonder and away from ourselves. It reveals the vastness of our life with him and something of the mystery of himself. Darkness is where our words fail but where, in silence, God's presence is most truly felt.[31]

Otto believed that the dark, or nonrational, aspect of religious experience "can be firmly grasped, thoroughly understood, and profoundly appreciated, purely in, with, and from the feeling itself."[32] It does not need to be subordinated to the rational aspect. For Otto this meant it does not need to be put into words to be meaningful.

This strong affirmation of the nonrational has, unfortunately, been confused by some modern-day theologians with the work of Otto's compatriot, theologian Friedrich Schleiermacher. The crucial difference, as Otto was very much aware, was that Schleiermacher saw consciousness of God's presence as the result of *inference* from a feeling of dependence within oneself. This was a process of simply reasoning from an experience entirely in oneself to a cause outside of oneself. Otto, however, saw consciousness of God's presence as resulting from *receptivity* to actual communication from God. Religious experience to Otto was a process of responding to an objective God outside of oneself with a feeling concerning him and what he has communicated, not just a feeling of one's inner self.

Otto's ideas were remarkably similar to Jonathan Edwards's regarding the base and the balance of religious experience. Edwards could have easily agreed with Otto's proposition that true religious experience is based on response to the communication of an objective God. He could also have heartily agreed with Otto's further affirmation that the nonrational is not subordinate to the rational and that they are equally essential parts of religious experience. To Otto, this meant that together they comprise, to use his favorite simile, the warp and woof of the complete fabric. Therefore, the nonrational should not be subordinated to the rational, but neither should it be left as a reality all its own. Rather, the two must be integrated.

An encounter with God can be deeply understood without translating it into rational categories. However, even though "something may be profoundly and intimately known in [the] feeling for the bliss it brings or the agitation it produces, and yet the understanding may find no concept for it,"[33] the understanding is not complete. The experience has meaning but not significance.[34] The emotional content needs to be related to a context, to something or someone outside of the person. As Otto says, it needs to be progressively charged with rational, moral, and cultural significance. Again, Edwards could have agreed, since he believed that true religious experience is always an integrated experience of reason and emotion and one that is moral to the core.[35]

I might say, "Oh, that was a meaningful experience!" But I must then interrogate the experience with questions like: "Is it reasonable?"—"Is it moral?"—"How does it fit into this culture?" The nonrational feeling need not be translated into rational categories, but it does need to be related to a rational, moral, cultural context. "It is reasonable and morally defensible to feel that way," is a conclusion I am sure both Edwards and Otto could have concurred in.

Jonathan Edwards and Rudolf Otto have given us an excellent framework for understanding religious experience. To them, a true religious experience is based on the subjective encounter of the objective reality of God. Further, the rational and nonrational components of the encounter are balanced, with neither being subordinate to the other. The nonrational is meaningful in and of itself, but must be given rational (as well as moral and cultural) significance.

Validation

From Edwards and Otto, we have a general understanding of a true religious experience. But how can we know that a specific religious experience is in fact true?

At one extreme are those who claim that true religious experience is self-validating, that is, beyond validation on any terms other than its own. Religious experience can be ratified only on the terms in which it is given, as a direct communication from God to a specific individual. It must be regarded as true, then, since it is directly from God. And it is in no need of any type of consensual confirmation, because it was intended only for the individual to whom it was given.

At the other extreme are those who take the person totally out of the validation process and merely check the soundness of the occurrence against an appropriate text in Scripture; we could call this Scripture-validating. For example, if I were to hear someone speak in tongues but there was no follow-up interpretation (as there should be, according to 1 Cor. 14:27), I would then immediately discount all claims that it was truly from God. If I were deeply biased, I would fail to note that in the absence of an interpreter the experience must be kept to oneself, but that it is not disqualified as a true religious experience (v. 28).

The Scripture-validating extreme is another manifestation of rationalistic bias. A religious experience is not validated as a personal experience, because it is assumed that God does not reveal his truths through human experience as such. Revelations in the past, like those recorded in the Old Testament, are not meant for our time. God allowed visions and healings only by a special dispensation, to

> establish the people of Israel and, through them, the Church of Christ. Then he withdrew this dispensation and the normal order was restored. . . . The Holy Spirit is not intended to be the giver of these experiences to men, but is only sent to give the conviction that they did happen. . . .
>
> One's relation to God, then, is not a matter of a divine-human encounter, of two realities coming into confrontation, but rather a one-way street of the Word of God slipping into man's mind and instructing this part of him.[36]

To avoid the extremes of self-validation and Scripture-validation of religious experience, we must include in the validation process the participation of a reference group and the description of personal experience. Dermot Lane asserts that "individual experiences must be tried and tested against the corporate experiences of the community. . . . Individuals as individuals cannot critically assess their own experiences without reference to some other group or community."[37] And, according to Jonathan Edwards, the distinguishing marks of the work of the Holy Spirit include personally descriptive signs such as (a) the breakdown of one's usual frames of self-consciousness, (b) esteem for Jesus Christ, (c) a high regard for the Bible, and (d) genuine love for God and for others.[38]

Lane is saying that one's religious reference group is the appropriate context for validating religious experience. It is also the proper context for relating the rational and nonrational aspects of the experience: "The community acts as a guide for understanding the significance of human experience."[39] I see this as a reference to the *meaning-significance distinction* developed earlier. Interestingly, the distinction appears to be encompassed in Lane's criteria for validation, which we will now look at.

Criteria

Lane lists twelve validation criteria, which I have modified and compressed into six. They are more specifically connected to religious experiences than Edwards's distinguishing marks of the work of the Holy Spirit, which could serve as more general criteria. The list has two parts, the first being a group of three criteria of adequacy. They are primarily concerned with meaning.

1. Meaningfulness—the experience complements ordinary human experience, so that it enriches our daily life.
2. Worthwhileness—the experience reaffirms our creatureliness and reassures our confidence in the value of existence.
3. Coherence—it is possible to express the nonrational meaning of the experience rationally, so that it can be given rational, moral, and cultural significance.

Second is a group of three criteria of appropriateness. These are primarily concerned with significance.

1. Worthiness—the transcendent object upon which the experience is focused is worthy of ultimate concern and total surrender.
2. Conversion—the person's life is transformed, in behavior as well as attitude.
3. Compatibility—the experience is in harmony with the person's religious reference group.[40]

These six criteria are similar to the seven criteria for existential validation (see chapter 1). The criteria of meaningfulness, worthwhileness, coherence, and worthiness correlate well with the five criteria pertaining to symbols in the process of existential validation. The two criteria pertaining to the co-investigator, transformation and communication, are almost identical to the criteria of conversion and compatibility on Lane's list.

Experiential Theology

Given the subjective nature of true religious experience (Edwards and Otto) and the qualitative nature of the validation criteria (Lane), the research methodology for validating religious experiences would have to be participant in nature (Giorgi, Colaizzi, and Van Leeuwen). Lane completely agrees: "The nature of human contact with the religious dimension . . . is such that it cannot be detached or controlled in laboratory-like circumstances."[41] To understand and validate an experience of the revelation of God, with all its ramifications and implications, requires the personal participation of the individual in the research process.

This approach to validating religious experience could be called experiential theology. The point is to get the person who has experienced the revelation personally involved in the process of validating it. One possibility would be to employ some sort of testing procedure, perhaps a correlational study comparing the person's responses on two different tests geared toward different aspects of the same experience. For example, to gain a better initial perspective on a person's tendency toward frequent, profound religious experiences, we might begin our research by administering the Intrinsic-Extrinsic Religious Orientation Scale[42] and the Religious Experience Episodes Measure (REEM).[43] These two instruments could help us determine whether the person has so completely internalized his or her faith that it has become interwoven throughout the fabric of the individual's personality (intrinsic orientation) and in turn predisposed the person to "deeper" religious experiences (high score on the REEM). The results would be rather speculative, but could lead the rest of the research in a more fruitful direction.

To get the high degree of personal involvement and participation that is needed throughout the existential validation of a religious experience, however, I recommend the phenomenological research method detailed in chapter 1. There would actually be a slight addition to the procedure, after the first five steps have been completed. At that juncture, there would be an accurate understanding of the experience on its own terms. The understanding would be in the form of a summary description of the experience and presumably contain in it both the meaning of the experience for the individual and its rational, moral, and cultural significance. The description would then be checked, in step 6, against the additional three criteria of adequacy and three criteria of appropriateness.

This proposal of a methodology for the validation of religious experience is just that—a proposal. It is not as yet tried and true. But there are other participant-observation approaches being devised that also remain to be tested.[44] These are exciting times for the integration of psychology and theology, as new methods continue to be developed and tried. I am especially hopeful that this version of experiential theology may prove to be a fruitful method for the expansion of our understanding of human-divine encounter.

The key to validation of a religious experience is the accurate understanding of what the experience is like for the individual—not what it should be like, but what it is like. Many studies take this point far too lightly, rushing to analyze data that do not accurately represent the experience. This is where the phenomenological method is a tremendous asset. It is also why, in considering the question of whether we should emphasize participant rather than detached observation when studying religious experience, I will unhesitatingly say yes.

In summary, the guidelines for a liberated theology, the recommendations for including all races and both sexes in the doing of theology, the consideration of the world view and nonrationality hermeneutical factors, and the development of an experiential theology for validating religious experience, all point clearly to the need for theological methods to be examined before facts that they produce are integrated. They also open up many new doors for communicating with God.

Notes

1. Cox, H. Theology: What is it? Who does it? How is it done? *The Christian Century* 97(29) (1980): 874–79.

2. Brown, R. M. Liberation theology: Paralyzing threat or creative challenge? In *Mission trends no. 4: Liberation theologies in North America and Europe,* ed. G. H. Anderson and T. F. Stransky. New York and Grand Rapids: Paulist and Wm. B. Eerdmans, 1979, pp. 3–24.

3. Wells, D. F., and Woodbridge, J. D. eds., *The evangelicals: What they believe, who they are, where they are changing,* rev. ed. Grand Rapids: Baker Book House, 1977.

4. Brown, Liberation theology, p. 4.

5. Cox, Theology, pp. 874–75.

6. Brown, Liberation theology, pp. 5–6.

7. Padilla, C. R. Liberation theology (II): An evaluation. *The Reformed Journal* 33(7) (1983): 14–18.

8. Ibid., p. 14.

9. This is a play on words and is not to be confused with "liberation theology" per se.

10. Anderson and Stransky, eds., *Mission trends no. 4.*

11. Bushnell, K. C. *God's word to women*. Reprinted. North Collins, N.Y.: Ray B. Munson, 1923, Pars. 12, 13, 375.

12. Ibid., par. 112.

13. Wolterstorff, N. The Bible and women: Another look at the "conservative" position. *The Reformed Journal* 29(6) (1979): 23–26.

14. Noll, M. Who sets the stage for understanding Scripture? *Christianity Today,* 24(10) (1980), p. 17.

15. Ibid.

16. Mickelsen, B., and Mickelsen, A. Does male dominance tarnish our translations? *Christianity Today* 22(23) (1979), p. 25.

17. Ibid., p. 29.

18. Johnson, C. B. *The psychology of biblical interpretation*. Grand Rapids: Zondervan, 1983, pp. 43-50.

19. Farnsworth, K. E.; Alexanian, J. M.; and Iverson, J. D. Integration and the culture of rationalism: Reaction to responses to "the conduct of integration," part 2. *Journal of Psychology and Theology* 11 (1983), p. 349.

20. Ibid., p. 351.

21. See L. J. Crabb, Jr. Biblical authority and Christian psychology. *Journal of Psychology and Theology* 9 (1981): 305–11; Guy, J. D., Jr. Affirming diversity in the task of integration: A response to "Biblical authority and Christian psychology." *Journal of Psychology and Theology* 10 (1982): 35–39.

22. Holmes, A. F. *Contours of a world view*. Grand Rapids: Wm. B. Eerdmans, 1983, chap. 9.

23. Johnson, *Psychology of biblical interpretation,* p. 103.

24. Wolterstorff, N. *Reason within the bounds of religion*. Grand Rapids: Wm. B. Eerdmans, 1976.

25. Hirsch, E. D., Jr. *Validity in interpretation*. New Haven, Conn.: Yale University Press, 1967, pp. 6–10, 258–64.

26. Lane, D. A. *The experience of God: An invitation to do theology*. New York: Paulist, 1981, pp. 12–13.

27. Gelpi, D. L. *Experiencing God: A theology of human emergence*. New York: Paulist, 1978, p. 5.

28. Lane, *Experience of God,* pp. 3, 4.

29. Cherry, C. *The theology of Jonathan Edwards*. Garden City, N.Y.: Doubleday, 1966, p. 167.

30. Hutch, R. A. Jonathan Edwards' analysis of religious experience. *Journal of Psychology and Theology* 6 (1978), p. 125.

31. These contrasts are taken primarily from R. Otto, *The idea of the holy: An inquiry into the non-rational factor in the idea of the divine and its relation to the rational,* trans. John W. Harvey, 2d ed. New York: Oxford University 1950; Appendix 11, *The mysterium tremendum,* in Robertson and Watts, pp. 220–21.

32. Otto, *Idea of the holy,* p. 34.

33. Ibid., p. 135.

34. "Failure to consider this simple and essential distinction has been the source of enormous confusion in hermeneutic theory." Hirsch, *Validity in interpretation,* p. 8.

35. Hutch, Jonathan Edwards, p. 130.

36. Kelsey, M. *Encounter with God: A theology of Christian experience*. Minneapolis: Bethany Fellowship, 1972, pp. 30–31.

37. Lane, *Experience of God,* pp. 10–11.

38. Hutch, Jonathan Edwards, p. 127.

39. Lane, *Experience of God,* p. 10.

40. Ibid., pp. 23–27.

41. Ibid., p. 27.

42. Robinson, J. P., & Shaver, P. R. eds., *Measures of social psychological attitudes*. Ann Arbor: Institute for Social Research, 1973, chap. 10.

43. Hood, R. W., Jr. Religious orientation and the report of religious experience. *Journal for the Scientific Study of Religion* 9 (1970): 285–91.

44. Malony, H. N. Religious experiencing: A phenomenological analysis of a unique behavioral event. *Journal of Psychology and Theology* 9 (1981): 326–34.

3

Integration Methodology

The manna story in Exodus 16 outlines a struggle that is basic to the human condition. It vividly portrays the continuous human struggle between not being satisfied and having enough. In psychological and theological terms, it is the struggle between trusting in human provision and trusting in God's provision. The story brings to life the difficulty we have in relating the human and the divine.

Integration is not automatic. It too is a story of struggle, much like the story of the nation of Israel having come out of Egypt into the wilderness and not as yet having arrived in Canaan. The integration story similarly involves, at an individual level, a tension between redemption and emancipation. In other words, we have been delivered out of slavery—the slavery of total reliance on ourselves—into the wilderness—the wilderness of learning how to rely completely on God. The integration problem is how to bring God's truths, from all areas of his creation, to bear on our redeemed but not fully emancipated lives.

One answer to the problem is critical integration.[1] This is an approach that takes basic Christian principles and applies them to psychology for the purpose of orienting one's life toward seeking first the kingdom of God. The method of critical integration is scrutiny from this Christian perspective of psychological theory, research, and practice, and the basic underlying assumptions of each. The result is the incorporation into one's thinking of those psychological theories, research findings, and procedures for application, that are compatible with Christianity.

Another possibility is embodied integration.[2] This approach conceptually relates psychology and theology and applies the results to everyday life. The purpose is to move beyond a conceptual kingdom-orientation, to an actually lived wilderness experience of the truths that have intellectually delivered one from bondage to oneself. The embodied integration method consists of verifying the soundness of the psychological and theological methodologies that generated the findings to be integrated, relating the findings to each other, and applying them in one's own life. The result of embodied integration is Christian living, in contrast to the result of critical integration, which is Christian thinking.

The similarities and contrasts of these two approaches will highlight two basic integration issues. Should theology be the guardian discipline for protecting the truth? And is integration complete when it is only intellectual, or should it be incarnational?

Critical Integration

Christian sociologist David Lyon has attached the word "critical" to integration to emphasize the role that a Christian perspective should play in a Christian's interaction with sociology, and by implication, with psychology.[3] The perspective is critical because it ferrets out the influence of non-Christian assumptions that steer research in non-Christian directions. Further, it provides guidelines for discerning which research findings God wants us to regard as true.

Christian World View

A Christian perspective is commonly referred to as a Christian world view. Basically, it is comprised of one's fundamental beliefs about the God/creation distinction and relationship arrived at in light of one's Christian commitment.[4] These beliefs are primarily, but not exclusively, drawn from the Bible, and some tend to be quite general.[5]

Although a world view is a conceptual framework for the process of setting limits and suggesting priorities, the process is also partially a preconceptual experience. In other words, it includes preverbal, prereflective feelings as well as verbal conceptions or thoughts. For example, my felt-sense of beauty, as an unreflected-upon expression of my deeply felt appreciation of God's creation, could be a significant factor in my acceptance of one psychological theory over another. In fact, it has been said that it is "unmistakably . . . a sense of beauty which moves us to prefer some theories to others, and even to heuristically commit ourselves to them even though as yet we have no clear conception of their consequences."[6]

The foundational components of a Christian world view are the biblical doctrines of creation, sin, redemption, and hope—the past, present, and future of the Christian faith. Taken all together they remind us of God's continuous acts of creation, our willful rebellion against our Creator (Upholder), and our redemption through his grace upon which is based our hope for the future.

As an example of the use of an individual world-view component, the doctrine of creation reminds us of our creatureliness, which reassures us that while we are not gods, we are not garbage either. Thus, we can have confidence in our self-worth without taking it to the extreme of self-worship. Another example would be the use of the doctrine of sin to reject a psychological theory of personality, education, or psychotherapy that espouses the "horticultural view of self." This is the view that assumes a person is filled with goodness that must be allowed just to ooze forth—like a rose unfolding from a rosebud—unburdened by any sort of limitation.

In choosing more specialized world-view components one finds a wide variety of possibilities. For this reason, Arthur Holmes points out the likelihood of more than a single Christian world view.[7] With that in mind, let us consider the specialized world-view components of relatedness, humanness, and separateness to help bring a Christian perspective to psychological theory, research, and practice, respectively.

Relatedness

We are relational beings.

> No man is an island, entire of itself; every man is a piece of the continent, a part of the main. If a clod be washed away by the sea, Europe is the less, as well as if a promontory were, as well as if a manor of thy friend's or of thine own were: any man's death diminishes me, because I am involved in mankind, and therefore never send to know for whom the bell tolls; it tolls for thee.[8]

It is not a question of who died. Everyone dies a little upon the death of a fellow human being. This kind of interrelatedness is referred to as the Hebrew dream of *shalom:* an all-inclusive wholeness with reciprocity of all the parts.[9] It is also the New Testament ideal for body life.

> The body is a unit, though it is made up of many parts; and though all its parts are many, they form one body. . . .
>
> If the foot should say, "Because I am not a hand, I do not belong to the body," it would not for that reason cease to be part of the body. And if the ear should say, "Because I am not an eye, I do not belong to the body," it would not for that reason cease to be part of the body. If the whole body were an eye, where would the sense of hearing be? If the whole body were an ear, where would the sense of smell be? But in fact God has arranged the parts in the body, every one of them, just as he wanted them to be. If they were all one part, where would the body be? As it is, there are many parts, but one body.
>
> The eye cannot say to the hand, "I don't need you!" And the head cannot say to the feet, "I don't need you!" On the contrary, those parts of the body that seem to be weaker are indispensable, and the parts that we think are less honorable we treat with special honor. And the parts that are unpresentable are treated with special modesty, while our presentable parts need no special treatment. But God has combined the members of the body and has given greater honor to the parts that lacked it, so that there should be no division in the body, but that its parts should have equal concern for each

other. If one part suffers, every part suffers with it; if one part is honored, every part rejoices with it. (1 Cor. 12:12, 15–26 NIV)

Humanness

Humans are unified beings, which implies individual wholeness in addition to corporate wholeness. Humans are also moral agents, which implies individual responsibility as well.

David Lyon puts humanness at the very center of both the biblical revelation and critical integration.[10] Christian philosopher Stephen Evans regards wholeness as the primary biblical emphasis concerning human beings.[11] And, according to Arthur Holmes, it is overwhelmingly clear in Scripture that God holds humans responsible.[12] It is safe to say, then, that humans are not reducible to less than whole persons and that personhood involves responsibility before God for the making of nonautonomous choices.

Psychology, if it is to provide an adequate picture of humanness, must be monitored to insure that basic Christian assumptions about personhood are not violated. Without a Christian perspective, the picture is just not complete.

> Someone has said that war is too important to be left to generals. So here we might say that the essential truth about personhood is too important to be left to the sciences. Though scientific knowledge may be tremendously important, one does not need to go to psychology textbooks to realize that one is a person and that to be a person is to be faced with decisions for which one is responsible. Anyone who honestly asks, "What shall I do with my life?" possesses the resources to understand what it is to be a person. And a person who possesses this understanding is at least intellectually ready for a confrontation with the Christian revelation in which the True Person makes himself known. For the biblical account of man's nature, origin, present status and future potential through God's redemptive activity is throughout an account of persons acting responsibly or irresponsibly in relationship to God and their fellow persons.[13]

Separateness

We are called-out beings: we are in the world, not of the world. According to Dutch theologian Hendrik Berkhof, Christians should therefore view the world as the One who called them out does.

> Through God's dealings with the world we get a glimpse of how He "views the world." In this sense a certain amount of "world view" is a part of faith. In the light of God's action Paul perceived that mankind is not composed of loose individuals, but that structures . . . are given us as a part of creaturely life and that these are involved, as much as men themselves, in the history of creation, fall, preservation, reconciliation, and consummation.[14]

Through Paul's eyes, God's view is that social structures are as integral a part of the world as are humans. Paul also saw a strong relationship between the structures and the fallen spiritual beings that influence the structures for evil—referred to by Paul as "the powers." It is because of the powers' evil-doing that we should separate ourselves from their influences. Berkhof tells us how.

> The believer does not flee the world, but he avoids deifying it. For him the world is "de-deified." In this sense there is a real place for a Christian avoidance of the world. The "weak" need to avoid certain realms of the world because the Powers who reign there would draw them away from their fellowship with their Lord.
>
> The strong can express this "avoidance of the world" in other ways, even by walking through the middle of its kingdoms, withstanding undaunted by their action and their very presence, like the young men in the fiery furnace. In so doing we must constantly remind ourselves: we do not belong to the nation, the state, the technique, the future, the money, but all this is ours, given us by God as means of living a worthy life before God and in fellowship with our neighbor.[15]

As Christians we must, through separateness from the world, "hold the Powers, their seduction and their enslavement, at a distance. . . . Our weapon is to stay close by Him and thus to remain out of the reach of the drawing power of the Powers."[16]

Psychological Theory

Much of modern psychological theory is based on fulfillment of the individual. In particular, the emphasis of self-theorists, such as

Fromm, Maslow, and Rogers, and the self-helpers who use their theories, is almost exclusively on the self. Their relentless individualism, or selfism, certainly runs counter to a Christian perspective that recognizes the person as a relational being.

Two recent books are very critical of the modern me-ism mania. *Psychology's Sanction for Selfishness* admonishes self-theorists for assuming that human motivation is based on personal needs and desires rather than concern for the welfare of others. The authors further claim that the problem is made worse by therapies that evolve from the theories prescribing self-expression, self-acceptance, and self-fulfillment as a cure-all.[17]

The other book, *Psychological Seduction,* criticizes the self-absorption that is the "good news" of the psychological "gospel."[18] As it turns out, however, it is really "bad news."

> We are forced to entertain the possibility that psychology and related professions are proposing to solve problems that they themselves have helped to create. We find psychologists raising people's expectations for happiness in this life to an inordinate level, and then we find them dispensing advice about the mid-life crisis and dying. We find psychologists making a virtue out of self-preoccupation, and then we find them surprised at the increased supply of narcissists. We find psychologists advising the courts that there is no such thing as a bad boy or even a bad adult, and then we find them formulating theories to explain the rise in crime. We find psychologists severing the bonds of family life, and then we find them conducting therapy for broken families.[19]

The point is a good one, however we must remember that the correlation between conducting therapy for families that are splitting up and also for those that have already split up, for example, does not prove causation. If, to further the example, psychologists are actually involving themselves more in the divorce than in the reconciliation of married couples, and they are also conducting therapy with an ever-increasing number of broken families, then we should show concern with the former and be sure that the latter is not feeding off the former. Just because they are related does not necessarily mean that one is causing the other.

Moral Development

Individualism is also a problem in a theoretical area of great interest to Christians: moral development. Dominating the field is the work of psychologist Lawrence Kohlberg. Originally, his theory was comprised of three general levels and six specific stages describing the development of moral reasoning.[20]

The third level is of concern here. Level III, the postconventional level, is where the person supposedly shakes loose from the external authority of accepted social standards. Moral judgment is based on autonomous, self-chosen principles. This is thought to be a higher level of moral development than the two lower levels.

Each level has two stages, so Stages Five and Six reveal how Level III itself develops. Since by the time Stage Five is reached moral reasoning is no longer accountable to a specific reference group, it begins to operate freely within the general confines of individual rights as agreed upon by the larger society. Any matter that falls outside those confines "progresses" further to the domain of personal values and opinion. This ushers in Stage Six, where moral reasoning is supposedly based solely on self-chosen ethical principles. These principles are not concrete moral rules, like the Ten Commandments, but highly abstract beliefs.

Through the years, Stage Six has been heavily criticized as elitist and opposed to the building of community. In addition, it has not held up empirically; longitudinal studies have failed to turn up people who have achieved Stage Six. Consequently, Stage Six is now being phased out. Kohlberg, lamenting the loss at a recent symposium, simply said, "Perhaps all the Sixth Stage persons of the 1960s had been wiped out, perhaps they had regressed, or maybe it was all my imagination in the first place."[21]

More recently, Kohlberg has refocused his attention on Stage Four, hoping to help people become good community members and good citizens. One could easily conclude that he is becoming quite Christian in his thinking. Moral beings are relational beings after all. We must, however, not jump to conclusions.

Upon closer inspection, it can be seen that Kohlberg is concerned only with form, and not at all with content.[22] His entire emphasis is on how someone reasons, not on what he or she reasons about. The theory is actually more about cognitive development than about moral development.

What Kohlberg assumes in his theory of cognitive development is that people develop from one cognitive ability to another—from one, it is further assumed, universal pattern of reasoning to another. Morality, then, is based on form, not content. Individual reasoning is king. There is no need whatsoever to be dependent on or answerable to a normative community—a community that supplies a standard for its members' morality.

Kohlberg does not seem to fare any better than the self-theorists do. In both cases, the process of critical integration ferrets out the individualistic bias of their underlying assumptions. I think the value of including relatedness in one's Christian world view is readily apparent. Now let us turn to another area of psychological endeavor.

Psychological Research

According to Stephen Evans, "It is fair to say that the rise of the human sciences in the twentieth century has been marked by the demise of the person. That is, there is a definite tendency to avoid explanations of human behavior which appeal to the conscious decisions of persons in favor of almost any impersonal factor."[23] There is a tendency to avoid viewing human beings as unified beings, irreducible to parts or disconnected processes, and particularly as moral agents, responsible to God for making non-autonomous choices.

In psychological research, the demise of personhood can be largely attributed to the prevalence of dehumanizing presuppositions. Individualism is one such presupposition, already discussed in connection with psychological theory, and there are many similar -isms that apply to psychological research. Chief among them are:

1. Reductionism—the whole is nothing but what is represented by a smaller part or the sum of all the parts. Man is nothing but . . .

2. Evolutionism—comparative research across species finds

similarities in anatomical structures and physiological functions, so behavioral processes must also be similar.

3. Behaviorism—a person is simply conditioned by the environment to respond in various ways that can be measured.

4. Determinism—behavior always has a prior cause. Freedom is an illusion.

Earlier we examined the tendency to reduce emotions to stimulus-response connections and cognitions to computerlike programs, and the reduction of entire persons to machines through a process called nothingbutism. We also looked at the toll reductionism is taking in broader cultural terms as well as in the education of students within the field of psychology.

Also we have been over in detail the negative effects of both evolutionism and behaviorism, noting that psychologists have gotten quite a bit of mileage out of speculations regarding the comparability of the thoughts and feelings of monkeys and men, and that such a degree of continuity between the two is irreconcilable from a biblical perspective. We have also looked at behaviorism's exaggerated emphasis on environmental factors and uncompromising commitment to measurement rather than meaning and deception rather than dialogue (see chap. 1).

Determinism

This presupposition is similar to reductionism in that the problem is one of degree. I doubt that any psychologist who agrees that humans have the ability to transcend environmental determinants and make self-determining choices would argue that it is not a limited ability. There are those psychologists, however, who claim that humans do not possess even a limited ability to transcend environmental determinants. That is determin*ism*.

Determinism, as a radical denial of freedom, has a variety of names: hard determinism; metaphysical determinism; moral determinism; unidirectional determinism. Regarding the latter, psychologist Albert Bandura has challenged its proponents who bend over backward to try to explain human behavior without the slightest reference to self-generated influences on behavior.

> One solution is to redefine the phenomenon out of existence. Self-directed change through personally arranged incentives [is] relabeled as . . . a stimulus signalling that a response [has] been executed. . . .
>
> The second, and more commonly used, solution is to execute a regress of causes. By locating a remote environmental factor that might affect self-reactions, self-generated influences are thereby converted into simple operants. . . . The organism thus becomes simply a repository of self-control responses waiting to be externally activated. . . . But causal regression is a no more convincing disposal of self-generated influences than is renaming, because for every environmental cause that is invoked, one can find a prior personal cause of that environment.[24]

Neither renaming nor causal regression offers an adequate explanation, according to Bandura. He has also challenged the central role of reinforcement in unidirectional determinists' thinking. Their assumption that reinforcement automatically and unconsciously shapes responses, making persons nothing more than "mechanical respondents to external stimuli," is flatly contradicted by Bandura's own empirical evidence. And, their argument that reinforcement history provides values and standards for behavior without any need for a personally initiated valuing process is also refuted by Bandura.

It is evident to me that the process of critical integration benefits from the internal critique of psychology by non-Christian psychologists just as much as by Christian psychologists—perhaps even more so. In the case of psychological research, the general tendency to repudiate the undiminished humanness of the human person is obvious for all to see.

Any Christian can call psychology into question from an external perspective, using a Christian world view either as salt of the earth or a city on a hill. In other words, one's Christian world view can make its presence felt either through interaction as a corrective or through separation as an alternative.

The city metaphor is precisely what I had in mind in chapter 1. It is also descriptive of Mary Van Leeuwen's recent book, that similarly proposes basic changes from a Christian perspective that would be a constructive alternative—a city on a hill—to mainline psychology.[25] Several other Christian psychologists have shown how a Christian world view can be used as a corrective through constructive interaction—as salt—with mainline psychology. Mark Cosgrove, for instance, has critiqued the work of B. F. Skinner from the standpoint of a Christian world view;[26] Malcolm Jeeves has applied Christian thinking to the values as well as dangers of studying animal behavior to learn more about human behavior;[27] and David Myers has done a series of inquiries into the complementary nature of Christian beliefs and a wide variety of psychological research findings.[28]

Psychological Practice

The third major area of psychological activity is practice. One of the most popular sub-areas of psychological practice, especially among Christians, is counseling. Because of its growing importance within the church, a critical integration of the counseling field with a Christian world view would certainly be appropriate.

The Christian world-view component that I regard as most relevant for integration in the area of counseling is separateness, the belief that Christians are called-out beings—in the world, not of the world.[29] The reason for the emphasis on separateness is the pervasive influence of the fallen spiritual beings known as the "powers." Christian counselors must find ways to stay away from the reach, the seduction, the enslavement of the "powers."

Yet I am surprised and somewhat alarmed at the number of Christian counselors who seem to have lost their sense of called-outness and have apparently given in to the ways of the world. It is difficult nowadays to discern any tangible differences between Christian and non-Christian counselors. The issue can perhaps be summarized by calling attention to the continuing shift of Christian counseling from an independent, church-sponsored service *ministry* to full participation in the professionally sanctioned service *industry*. This is movement into the world on the world's terms, and it brings Christian counselors directly within the reach of the "powers" and their influence through the structures of secular professionalism.

Professionalism

In his commencement address at Harvard University a few years ago, Russian author Aleksandr Solzhenitsyn decried the legalistic life, which only requires one to do what is right from a legal point of view. Nothing more is necessary; voluntary self-restraint and personal sacrifice are practically nonexistent. This mentality, when taken up by the Christian counselor, translates into abiding by the ethics of the profession as the ultimate requirement for professional conduct. I would call this professionalism.[30]

The issue concerns the lordship of one's professional life. Will it be a legalistic life or one that is more—and less—than that, one that is committed to the lordship of Jesus Christ at every point?

Focusing our attention on counselor preparation and counseling practice, should the primary goal of a Christian counselor education program be certification by a professional body? Should the primary goal of an individual Christian counselor be licensure by the state? These are not bad goals as such. They are good, but not good enough.

A Christian world view holds within it a warning that we must not win the battle, but lose the war. This means that Christian counselors must earn recognition as competent professionals, but the real battle, the war, is for the redemption of persons and institutions. It is a spiritual war that confronts the Christian counselor, an engagement of the "powers" to de-deify the educational and service structures of the counseling profession. A strategy must be worked out to subordinate these structures, not to the sovereignty of the profession, but to the lordship of Jesus Christ.

Any strategy for relating a Christian world view to Christian counselor education programs must address their organizational administrative structure, structures for articulating personnel policies and for implementing procedures for carrying them out, and academic structures for deciding the content of their course offerings. The result should be more than wisdom, might, and riches: let them boast in administrative decisionmaking and personnel policies and procedures based on *loving-kindness,* a curriculum that teaches concern for *justice,* and an educational community where caring relationships foster *righteousness* in each community member (cf. Jer. 9:23–24).

Whereas more is required of Christian educational programs than their secular counterparts, less may very well be required of Christian counselors than non-Christian counselors. It may not be advisable, for example, for the Christian counselor to participate in a licensing system that limits the number of counselors and thereby inflates the cost of counseling services. It must not be forgotten that it is the Christian's responsibility to minister to those in need regardless of the circumstances (e.g., those too poor to pay).

Also, rather than charge a fee for counseling services that is based on what the traffic will bear, which would certainly be in compliance with the professional code of ethics, the Christian counselor may need to think seriously about what the selfless sacrifice referred to by Solzhenitsyn might entail. Perhaps a sliding scale based on ability to pay should be used. Or perhaps the counselor should have independent financial support, which would allow for just a token fee or elimination of the fee altogether.

Probably the best strategy for bringing one's counseling practice under the lordship of Christ is to establish a reference group of believers as the locus of one's professional accountability. This would be a Christian forum for prayerful discussion and discernment about such things as professional licensing and alternate fee structures. The group would be a ministry of the church and composed of both professional peers and knowledgeable lay persons.[31] The agenda of the group would include illumination of areas of professional activity that do not appear to be compatible with a Christian world view and support and encouragement for the counselor in his or her commitment to deal with them.[32]

In summary, critical integration confronts psychology in all of its manifestations and calls into question such dehumanizing and nonkingdom-oriented presuppositions as individualism, determinism, and professionalism. In addition, a Christian world view that affirms persons as relational, unified, responsible, and called-out beings provides the Christian with workable guidelines for incorporating results of psychological theorizing and research and professional expectations regarding psychological practice into his or her thinking.

However, the process is actually more of an incorporating of one truth or set of truths into another than a true integrating or blending of the two. Therefore, since Christian world view is the central focus, critical integration seems to give priority to the discipline of theology over all the other disciplines. Further, the emphasis is almost exclusively on Christian thinking. The two basic integration issues—Should theology be the guardian discipline for protecting the truth? Is integration complete when it is only intellectual?—are answered in the affirmative.

Embodied Integration

The other main approach to integration, embodied integration, does not elevate theology to a position above the other disciplines, nor does it restrict the scope of integration to the intellectual. It is an emphasis on all the disciplines equally and on Christian living at least as much as on Christian thinking.

Embodied integration is further differentiated from critical integration in that it focuses on the mechanics of research methodologies and is therefore scientific in its orientation. Critical integration, as we have noted, focuses on the assumptions that underlie research methodologies, which makes it a more philosophical orientation. Another difference is that critical integration looks for specific psychological conclusions that are incompatible with a more general Christian world view; embodied integration looks for specific psychological and theological conclusions that are comparable with each other. The emphasis of the former on points of tension stands in sharp contrast with the emphasis of the latter on points of similarity.

To summarize, the two integration processes relate very differently to research methods (scientific orientation vs. philosophical orientation), psychological conclusions (points of similarity vs.

points of tension), and the extent of implementation of the conclusions (Christian living vs. Christian thinking). The differences in relating to research methods and psychological conclusions, however, need to be clarified. Regarding research methods, it should be noted that because of its focus on the mechanics of research, embodied integration may at times include recollecting and/or reanalyzing data. Critical integration, on the other hand, being strictly a review of the assumptions underlying the research, would not. In other words, the contrast can be seen more precisely as doing research versus reviewing research.

The same contrast pertains to the two integrative approaches to psychological conclusions. We have described critical integration as a process of (a) scrutiny from a Christian perspective of psychological theory, research, and practice, and the underlying assumptions of each; and (b) incorporation into one's thinking of those psychological theories, research findings, and procedures for application that pass the test. Reinterpretation of research findings that are not consistent with a Christian world view into terms that are, so they can then be incorporated into one's thinking would be an addition to this definition.[33] If, however, the findings were based upon faulty data, or if the analysis of the data was inadequate, then any review of psychological conclusions, with or without reinterpretation, will be severely compromised.[34] Clearly, regenerating or reanalyzing the data (doing research) is at times a much-needed alternative to simply reviewing or, in addition, reinterpreting the conclusions.

The critical integration process of reviewing assumptions and conclusions, perhaps reinterpreting conclusions, and then incorporating conclusions into one's thinking can easily miss errors in the methodology and the original data that might well be picked up in the embodied integration process. It is obvious, therefore, that critical integration can be too far removed from the data. The reason, according to Michael DeVries, is its systems-analytic approach to organizing psychological concepts within a Christian framework, a process that relies almost totally on the logical coherence of one's Christian world view.

> It . . . fails to lend any certainty about the [truth] of the world-view presuppositions themselves. The validity of those presuppositions depends upon the theological/philosophical context from which *they* arise. World-view thinking seems to identify the validity of a Christian starting point in the sciences with logically-qualified propositions and their power to logically systematize concepts in psychology. Missing from "world-view" approaches to psychology by Christian thinkers is precisely the "world" pole of the hyphenated idea. Considerable attention has been given to the construction of a logically coherent *view,* but the "world" does not enter the discussion as "phenomenon" or as "reality," but only as concept to be systematized in terms of its "contents" qua concept.[35]

It is exactly this problem that embodied integration is designed to remedy. It connects with the "world" at both ends of the process: collecting and analyzing data, and applying the results to everyday life. And it connects both psychology *and* theology with the real world, which brings each one out of its own little world as the exclusive context for the validation of its conclusions as truth.

The most basic difference between the two integrative approaches boils down to emphasizing the "world" pole as opposed to the "view" pole. The emphasis carries through the entire process in both cases. For each the process has two main stages. In critical integration, the emphasis on conceptualization is readily apparent in the review stage and also in the incorporation stage. Embodied integration is comprised of the relation stage and the application stage. More specifically, they can be referred to as conceptual relation and personal application. Emphasis on the lived-world is easily recognized in the latter stage. It must be noted, however, that conceptual relation requires the regeneration or reanalysis of data referred to above, for its world-emphasis to be evident.

Conceptual Relation

I have already described embodied integration as a process of verification, relation, and application. This means that truth-claims discovered through reading Scripture or experiencing religious phenomena and researching human experience or reviewing psychological literature must be verified for their accuracy and related to each other before they can be applied in one's life. Verification and relation together are the first, conceptual relation stage of embodied integration.

Another way to describe the embodied integration process is "critique (and possible correction), comparison, and commitment." Corresponding psychological and theological facts are (a) critiqued for methodological-hermeneutical soundness and perhaps corrected through the regeneration and/or reanalysis of data, (b) compared with each other for degree of similarity, and (c) committed to as truths in one's own life. Again, conceptual relation is comprised of the first two, critique and comparison. It is interesting to note that whereas the first stage of critical integration may or may not include the reinterpretation of psychological conclusions, the first stage of embodied integration may or may not include the regeneration/reanalysis of either psychological or theological data.

The verification, or critique, aspect of conceptual relation is the methodological starting point. Any psychological and theological facts that we may want to integrate were determined by the methodologies that produced them. If the research was faulty, then the results are too: they are artifacts rather than facts. Therefore, to get integration off to a good start, we need to be able to recognize "good" psychology and "good" theology, or put ourselves in touch with those who can.[36] For integration to proceed, it must be established that the facts to be integrated are based on sound research methods. If we have to disqualify either the psychological facts or the theological facts, then we have the option of revising the methodology by regenerating or reanalyzing the data. Otherwise, integration is irrelevant and should not proceed.

Relation, or comparison, is the other aspect of conceptual relation. After the methodological-hermeneutical verification is completed, the facts from the two different disciplines must be compared to see how closely they correspond, or can be made to correspond, so they can be combined into a single idea. There are two approaches: manipulation and correlation. Manipulation involves determining whether either the psychological facts or the theological facts can be subsumed by their counterpart or recast in its terms. Correlation involves recognizing that the facts substantially agree or are at least complementary.

There are three manipulation and two correlation models. The Credibility Model subsumes psychology under theology; the Convertibility Model does just the reverse; and the Conformability Model recasts psychology into theology. The Compatibility Model points out how psychology and theology substantially agree, and the Complementarity Model acknowledges that they are at least complementary.[37]

Before proceeding we should note that there is some degree of conflict over whether models are an appropriate focus in the first place. Michael DeVries, for example, has the same complaint about models that he has about the world-view approach,[38] and I have taken this into consideration in presenting the embodied integration approach as an alternative. DeVries's criticism is that models are too far removed from concrete reality, that they rely on thinking about phenomena to the exclusion of actually coming into contact with phenomena through firsthand experience. The models we will examine, however, are only the middle component of an overall integrative process that connects with the lived-world on both sides, through verification and application.

There is also a fair degree of choice among competing models. Some of the more contemporary models are presented in table 1, in parallel relationship to my five models. Although space prevents my expanding on the alternative models, I should point out their self-contained, conceptual nature, which makes them vulnerable to DeVries's criticism above.

Also, note the gaps in the columns in table 1. This means that my five models comprise the most complete set. It is interesting, however, that while Carter's models are a renaming of theologian H. Richard Niebuhr's Christ and culture categories,[43] he does not utilize Niebuhr's "Christ above Culture" category, which he could

Table 1

The Parallel Relationships among Contemporary Conceptual Relation Models

	Carter[39]	Collins[40]	Evans[41]	Everett and Bachmeyer[42]
1. **Credibility**	Scripture against Psychology	Spoiling the Egyptians	Limiters of Science (Territorialists)	Reduction
2. **Convertibility**	Scripture of Psychology	—	Reinterpreters of the Person (Compatibilists) (Capitulators)	Reduction
3. **Conformability**	—	Rebuilding	—	—
4. **Compatibility**	Scripture Parallels Psychology (Correlation) Scripture Integrates Psychology	Railroad Track Integrated Models	—	Addition
5. **Complementarity**	Scripture Parallels Psychology (Isolation)	Levels of Analysis	Limiters of Science (Perspectivalists)	Translation

call "Scripture above Psychology" and which would match up with my Conformability Model. But because of the criticisms that have been made against Niebuhr's "Christ Transforms Culture" and "Christ against Culture" categories (Carter's Scripture Integrates Psychology and Scripture against Psychology Models), I would hesitate to use his categories as my conceptual relation models even as much as Carter already does.[44]

Let us now turn to a brief description of each of the five conceptual relation models to see how each model would either manipulate one or the other similar psychological and theological finding, or would correlate them, so they could be combined into a single idea for application in one's life. We will use the same findings in each case: *our behavior shapes our attitudes,* and *where our treasure is there will our heart be also*. And, let us assume that the methodological-hermeneutical verification of these two findings has been completed.

Credibility Model

The Credibility Model recognizes psychological findings only if they can be subsumed under theological findings. Psychological concepts are seen as secular concepts and therefore must be screened through the filter of Scripture to give them credibility. The model also gets its name from the fact that affirmation of such a process gives Christian psychologists an opportunity to enhance their personal credibility within the evangelical subculture.

According to this model, no psychological finding, regardless of its empirical support, will be accepted as truth if it conflicts with the teaching of Scripture. Christian psychologist Lawrence Crabb is one among many strong advocates of this position.[45] Taking the model to its extreme, one would accept as true only those psychological findings that can actually be found in the Bible. This is all right—though it severely limits the scope of integration—provided the psychological findings are not distorted so as to match Bible verses and the discipline of psychology retains its own identity.

The larger problem with the Credibility Model concerns theological imperialism. In other words, theology has assumed functional control over psychology. It is not the Bible that is in control of psychology, but another discipline—theology. The Bible is an object to be studied, and theology is the discipline for studying it. They are in two different categories; theology and psychology are in the same category, both being disciplines for study not objects of study. To manipulate a psychological finding to fit the Bible as a filter, then, is clearly a confusion of categories. Further, the resulting theological imperialism, by claiming that theological findings are superior to, or automatically "truer" than psychological findings, regardless of the topic and in spite of evidence to the contrary, makes a mockery of the additional claim that all truth is God's truth and he is the Creator and Sustainer of all creation.

When trying to relate into a single idea a psychological finding and a theological finding that do not have a sufficient degree of similarity, and in fact actually begin to look as though they are in conflict, there are two choices: one or the other is true, or they are both false. They cannot both be true if they disagree with each other. Nor is the theological finding automatically the true one. What one must do is go back and reverify the methodological/hermeneutical procedures that were involved in arriving at each conclusion. If this does not resolve the issue, then integration cannot proceed.

I must emphasize that I am not calling the Bible into question. I am calling human interpretations of it—theology—into question. There are those, however, who will not make the distinction (I call this "hardening of the categories") and who cannot tolerate the uncertainty of rechecking the theological as well as the psychological conclusion. Such persons are afraid that to have an open mind is to have an empty one. The problem is dogmatism: an unqualified certainty that the two disciplines are in hierarchical relationship, with theology automatically at the top, and an intolerance of ambiguity.[46]

If the problems of theological imperialism, confusion of categories, hardening of categories, and dogmatism can be moderated, then the Credibility Model can be useful in relating similar psychological and theological findings such as "behavior shapes our attitudes" and "where our treasure is there will our heart be also."

First, the model would prescribe a careful exegesis of Matthew 6:21 to insure that "treasure" is the same as "behavior" and "heart" is the same as "attitudes." If they are not, then the finding that behavior shapes attitudes will not be accepted as true, regardless of how many times it has been replicated. In that case, Matthew 6:21 can become part of one's approach to life on its own, without a psychological counterpart. That is fine; we just cannot technically call it integration.

If, however, it is found that the terms are equivalent, then the second step would be to bring the psychological under the umbrella of the theological. In other words, the combination of the two will be expressed in theological terms: what we treasure most affects us to the core of our being (our heart). We are now ready to apply it personally in our lives.

Convertibility Model

The Convertibility Model revises theological findings from the perspective of psychological findings, which reverses the emphasis of the Credibility Model. This model can be especially useful in studying religious experiences, by utilizing psychological insights to disentangle the human from the divine. By filtering the theological through the psychological, we can discern what psychological factors naturally accompany true religious experience (see chap. 2) as well as what theological cloaks-for-ignorance are misrepresenting ordinary human experience. The work of British psychiatrist William Sargant on the physiology of religious conversion is a shining example of the revision of simple theological explanations into more complex theological/psychological ones.[47]

The converting of totally theological explanations into partially psychological explanations can, however, get out of hand. For example, when it is difficult to explain an event accurately in theological terms, it can be very tempting to dive like a duck momentarily below the theological level and return to the surface with a whole mouthful of psychological explanations. But the diving-duck routine does not really help explain the event. It just displaces the problem to another level.[48]

As with the previous model, the larger problem with the Convertibility Model concerns imperialism. When psychology assumes more than just partial functional control over theology, it becomes psychological imperialism. This phenomenon is fairly common among religiously oriented non-Christian psychologists, and it usually takes one of two forms. One is the manipulation of theology by psychologizing theological findings. It involves, for example, interpreting all biblical references to sexual intimacy in terms of the Freudian theory of sexuality. When no room is left in any of the interpretations for the spiritual side of human nature, then we have "rearranged the revelation," in the words of French lay theologian and social critic Jacques Ellul.[49]

The other form of converting theology to psychology is demythologizing theological findings. Demythologizing is an approach to biblical stories that disregards them as historical fact and values them only as myths that reveal ancient folklore and universal psychological principles. The theological meanings of the details of the stories are irrelevant, because the music behind the words is all that matters. Consider Rollo May's classic rendering of "the myth of Adam" as a "fall upward":

> If we . . . look at the myth of Adam as the writers of Genesis presented it, we find . . . [it] portraying the birth of human consciousness. . . . Under the "benevolent dictatorship" of God, Adam and Eve exist in the Garden of Eden in a state of naive, prehuman happiness. . . . But what do they gain as they bid goodbye to Eden? They gain differentiation of themselves as persons, the beginnings of identity, the possibility of passion and human creativity. And in place of the naive, non-responsible dependencies of infancy, there is now the possibility of loving *by choice,* relating to one's fellowman because one wants to, and hence with responsibility. The myth of Adam is, as Hegel put it, a "fall upward."[50]

I am convinced that the diving-duck procedure and all forms of psychological imperialism must be avoided. The psychologizing and demythologizing of theology have no place in the integration of psychology and theology. If the Convertibility Model functions as it is intended, then psychological findings and theological findings can be related on a fairly equal basis.

In relating the psychological finding that behavior shapes attitudes and the theological finding that where your treasure is your heart is, the Convertibility Model would look for the psychological significance of the theological statement. In other words, it would see behavior as the intent of the word "treasure" and attitudes as being the intended meaning of "heart." It would then combine the two statements into a single idea that would prevent treasure specifically from being spiritualized away by referring to heavenly thoughts rather than earthly actions. The idea, then, would be in behavioral terms: what we do is a major determinant of the formation of attitudes and the changing of attitudes. That idea, or one like it, can now be applied in our everyday lives.

Conformability Model

This model reconsiders psychological findings from the perspective of more general theological findings, or a Christian world view. It is actually the review stage of the critical integration process. It is through the Conformability Model that critical integration can be assimilated by and become an integral part of the embodied integration process.

Because the psychological findings must conform to a Christian world view, there is a filtering process in the Conformability Model that makes it similar to the Credibility Model. There are differences, however. The Credibility Model, for instance, relies strictly on Scripture, and if possible, on specific verses of Scripture. In contrast, a Christian world view need not rely entirely on Scripture, and it tends to be rather general in nature.

Also, if the psychological and theological findings are in conflict, then the Credibility Model will simply reject the psychological finding. The Conformability Model, on the other hand, has as an alternative the option of reinterpreting the psychological finding to bring it into line with the Christian world view. This is the approach advocated by Christian psychologist Ronald Koteskey.[51] Even though reinterpretation is possible, it is not usually necessary (note my earlier suggestion that it is merely an addition to the critical integration process). The Conformability Model also rejects conflicting psychological findings when they flatly disagree with the Christian world view; and when the disagreement is not so obvious, the psychological finding is just called into question for further discussion. An excellent example—without the added manipulation of reinterpretation—is Mark Cosgrove's analysis of B. F. Skinner's behaviorism.[52]

The problems this model has in common with the Credibility Model and the review stage of critical integration must of course be overcome. They mainly include theological imperialism and the missing of errors in methodology and original data. Reinterpretations of psychological findings to bring them into accord with a Christian world view, for example, need to be kept to a minimum. This step, along with the willingness to call into question for further discussion those psychological findings that may or may not conflict with a Christian world view, rather than automatically rejecting them, should adequately moderate theological imperialism. And, the verification step in the embodied integration process should solve the problem of not recognizing errors in the research from which the findings came.

So the Conformability Model is in a relatively comfortable position for relating the two statements: "behavior shapes attitudes," and "where your treasure is your heart is." The first task is to compare the psychological finding, "behavior shapes attitudes," with a Christian world view. If they are in harmony, then a single idea can be developed from the two statements. The idea might be something like this: "Because humans are responsible beings, their lives are determined in large part by their own behavior." This idea, or a similar one, is now ready for personal application.

Compatibility Model

The Compatibility Model relates psychological and theological findings that clearly seem to be saying the same thing. The process of correlating them is very straightforward: they are given equal footing, then closely examined to see how compatible they really are, and then combined into a single new idea that represents them both equally. An example of two findings that can be correlated in this way are psychoanalyst Erich Fromm's "marketing orientation" concept—leading one's life as though he or she were a commodity on the market to be bought[53]—and Christ's strikingly similar reference to polishing the outside of the cup (cf. Matt.

23:25). In both cases there is an overriding concern about image and making a good impression, and in neither case is there a need for any kind of manipulation.

Theologian Thomas Oden has listed several pairs of findings from human-science-oriented psychology and experiential theology that are full of possibilities. He provides a parallel listing of a number of quotations from leaders of the early pietistic movement and the modern encounter culture, as in table 2.

Table 2

Oden's Parallel Findings

Pietistic Movement	**Encounter Culture**
Shun the very appearance of affectation. Let your words and your manner be perfectly natural. Do not . . . speak in borrowed nor hackneyed terms, lest it should become a merely formal exercise, and consequently a deceptive one.—*Newstead,* 1843	Words are special culprits in the effort to avoid personal confrontation.—*Schutz,* 1967
When a happy correspondence between the outward walk and inward piety of believers is discovered, which can be known only by the disclosure of the interior life, we are not only prepared to comfort, encourage and strengthen one another, but form an intimacy of the holiest nature, a union of the strongest character—*Rosser,* 1855	Where all is known and all accepted . . . further growth becomes possible. . . . To his astonishment, he finds that he is more accepted the more real that he becomes.—*Rogers,* 1970
Tell your experience; and tell your conflicts; and tell your comforts. As iron sharpeneth iron, as rubbing of the hands maketh both warm, and as live coals maketh the rest to burn, so let the fruit of society be mutually sharpening, warming, and influencing.—*Rosser,* 1855	To discover that a whole group of people finds it much easier to care for the real self than for the external facade is always a moving experience.—*Rogers,* 1970.[54]

Because of the ease of just lining up conclusions, as Oden has, this model is commonly misused. If the surface agreement of the two findings is taken no further than their casual alignment, with no close examination to check the degree of their compatibility, the result could be a marriage that does not last. An engaged-engagement process (the relation stage) is crucial for a long-term and deepening life together (the application stage).

Another problem with the model arises when one assumes that the synthesis, or the combination, of two findings into a new idea produces a truth that is truer than either of the two findings by itself. Perhaps this is what Aaron had in mind when he rebelled against the only, invisible God of all creation by creating by himself a golden bull so the Israelites could have another, visible god. By then trying to baptize his creation through offerings to the Lord, he seems to have been trying to combine the best of two very different worlds into something that was better than either. This is just as wrong as combining two synonymous findings into a single new idea and assuming that it is truer than the findings by themselves. "If something is true in the first place, . . . it cannot become truer, even though one's confidence in it and commitment to it as truth can become stronger by finding the same truth in other disciplines."[55]

If the conceptual relation process is relatively free of the two problems just discussed, then combining "behavior shapes attitudes" and "where your treasure is your heart is" becomes a matter of one's imagination. How could these two findings be expressed as a new idea that represents both equally? One possibility would be: "whatever one is most consistently involved in is what one will become." The next stage is personal application.

Complementarity Model

This model relegates psychological and theological findings to different but related levels of description. Since each discipline has its own perspective, and its findings are expressed in such dissimilar language, the job of the Complementarity Model is to show that they are not only different but also related in some way. If it can be shown that the findings are referring to the same thing only in different ways, then their complementary nature becomes evident. The process of correlating the findings, then, is simply a matter of recognizing two equally valid but different views of the same phenomenon. There is no need to combine them into a single idea, as in the other models. Rather, the one that is more personally relevant can be applied directly in one's life.

The other correlation model, the Compatibility Model, lines findings up horizontally and treats them equally. The Complementarity Model, however, layers them vertically and locates each type of finding at a particular level. Richard Bube, a Christian who is very active in integrating Christianity and science in general, has described the levels in table 3.

Table 3

Bube's Levels of Description

Object of Study	Process of Study
God	Theology
Society	Sociology
Man	Anthropology and Psychology
Animals	Zoology
Plants	Botany
Cells	Biology
Nonliving Matter	Chemistry and Physics[56]

Each level has its own story to tell. Theology, for example, tells the who and why story, and psychology tells the what and how story. Note that because Bube's description of the levels has theology at the top—the theology story being of a higher order than the psychology story because of its concentration on the more personal questions of who and why—we have a hierarchical relationship between psychological and theological findings. This is not, however, the same situation we had in the Credibility and Conformability models.

Although theological findings are presumed to be "higher" than psychological findings, they are not presumed to be truer. All that is intended, according to the chief proponent of this model, Donald MacKay, is that the theological findings presuppose the psychological findings and reveal their significance in fresh categories.[57]

For example, if a psychologist were conducting long-term research on the personality development of a person who suddenly experiences new meaning and direction in life, how would the psychologist explain it? Probably as some combination of sociocultural formative influences, physiological concomitants of the emotional side of the experience, and behavioral changes that can be associated with the person's stage of life and predisposing personality characteristics. But if the psychologist failed to entertain the possibility of the occurrence of a religious conversion, would it mean that he or she was not thorough enough, that the psychological analysis should have included something more? Not at all. Any tacked-on spiritual language would add nothing to the psychological account of the event.

If we are convinced, however, that the redirection of the person's life did in fact result from a conversion to Christ, then we have another complete explanation of the event. Again, it is not just a footnote to some other explanation. According to MacKay, "It is rather the point or significance of what is there—something we find by starting all over again and describing the very same situation in different, but equally justifiable and illuminating categories."[58]

Typically, the theological findings are more general than and give a broader perspective to the psychological findings. The benefit a psychological finding may receive from a theological finding is that the latter is an additional interpretation of the phenomenon itself, not a reinterpretation of the psychological interpretation of the phenomenon. This provides a more complete understanding, not a different one.

It is clear that the Complementarity Model allows each discipline to give an exhaustive description of the phenomenon in its own terms exclusively, without the help of another discipline's description *at that level*. It is this ability to let findings retain their own language, to stand without reinterpretation, that makes this model the most popular model among natural scientists. In psychology, it is especially popular among psychologists with a similar, laboratory-experimentation orientation. Malcolm Jeeves is a prime example.[59]

As is true with the other models, there can be problems with this one. For example, although it is not a major problem, there can be a polarization of the disciplines. That is, psychologists and theologians can get so wrapped up in telling their own stories that they fail to interrogate and correct each other's methods, as we have seen. Others have more sweepingly criticized the Complementarity Model for the methodological isolation of science in general from theology.[60]

In addition, theological imperialism is a strong possibility if the two disciplines are not encouraged to illuminate each other's findings. Thus far, the Complementarity Model has been used for the illumination and enrichment of psychological findings by theological findings far more than the other way around.

Assuming that methodological isolation and theological imperialism are not big problems, then the conceptual relation process is completed by making a simple decision. Which is more relevant for me, the fact that behavior shapes attitudes or the fact that where your treasure is your heart is? Which is the better way of saying it for me? All I need to do is pick one and live it.

Personal Application

The biblical emphasis is on receiving and responding, on knowing God as well as knowing about God. It is on doing not hearing only (James 1:22), on being a disciple as well as being a believer (1 Thess. 4:1–12). This is the reason that I have included an experiential (walking with God) stage along with the intellectual (talking with God) stage in the embodied integration process. Personal application is the necessary completion of the conceptual relation stage.

Application in one's life of the product of one of the conceptual relation models is what critical integration prepares for but does not prescribe. In other words, critical integration ends up with a Christian orientation toward something: it results in Christian thinking. Embodied integration, on the other hand, results in action, not orientation—in Christian living, not just Christian thinking. The goal of critical integration is orthodoxy. The goal of embodied integration is orthopraxy.

The application stage is the end and also the beginning of wholehearted integration. It is the dawning, or breaking, the day of either the embodied methodology alone or a combination of the critical and embodied methodologies—for example, moving from the comparison of concepts from different disciplines, through the clarification of the affinity of those concepts with a Christian world view, and into personal conviction and commitment to action. Wholehearted integration is the word made flesh, as Jesus himself was the Word made flesh. This is more than just an analogy. Wholehearted integration is the literal following of Jesus in both word and deed.

Wholehearted integration is, in a word, incarnational. God's truth lives through us as we live as Jesus lived. The application stage is the process of following Jesus by living what we intellectually understand to be God's truths as his framework for interpreting our experience and guidelines for making responsible choices.[61] And this is a *life-long process.* Integration is never finished.

Wholehearted integration is also a corporate affair. Both understanding truth intellectually and living truth are best done within a group of believers. Although research does not necessarily need to be done in the context of a group of believers, the process of discerning truth in Scripture should not be done in isolation. In addition, the support and encouragement of the church are essential as we try to live as Jesus lived in a sinful world.

Let us take a closer look at the actual process of personal application. Let us assume that the conceptual relation work has been done, and with the help of the Compatibility Model, for example, I have arrived at the conclusion that if I live for my career it will become my calling. This is an imaginative combination of "behavior shapes attitudes" and "where your treasure is your heart is," and is based on my knowledge of the psychology of careers and the theology of calling.

I know, for instance, that devotion to one's work life can be so intense and uncompromising that it can define the overall direction and meaning of one's entire life. And I also know that in the New Testament, "calling" is a technical term for the totality of the process of salvation. God is the caller, and we are the called (cf. Rom. 9:24; 11:29; 1 Cor. 1:9; 7:15, 20; Gal. 5:8; Eph. 4:1; 1 Thess. 5:24)—and this includes discipleship (Rom. 1:7) and citizenship in the kingdom of God (1 Thess. 2:12).[62] My calling is to follow Jesus as a citizen of his kingdom. My calling is to live up to my new name—"Christ-ian"—in other words, to be worthy of Christ. How, then, can I apply this knowledge in my life?

First, what I would *not* do:

1. Deny personal responsibility for my career-related decisions, releasing myself from all possible anxiety by expecting God just to call me.

2. Deny the necessity of considering my values, abilities, and interests in making decisions about a career, relying instead on the feeling of comfort and assurance I get from my sense of calling.

3. Choose one career as my career for life, as my calling. In short, I would not equate calling and career in either thought or action. Certainly God leads me and does so with definiteness in all areas of my life, including leading me into a specific career. I should not, however, say that he called me to that career.

Second, what I *would* do.

1. Take personal responsibility for my career-related decisions by including my values, abilities, and interests in the decision-making process.

2. Plan my career so that it is subordinated to the lordship of Jesus Christ, by including accountability to a body of believers in my career-related decisions and being open to the Holy Spirit's leading regarding possible career changes.

3. Take steps to insure that my career (or occupation) supports but does not determine the overall meaning and direction of my

life (or vocation): for example, include my family as voting members in any opportunity to change locations because of a job offer and turn down any overture for advancement that would redefine the centrality of my family in my life.

There are, of course, many ways to keep career from becoming calling, from becoming the main focus of life in place of Jesus and the example of his life on earth. But it is impossible to overemphasize the importance of this distinction in some people's lives. To mention a case in point, I was contacted not long ago on a radio talk-show by a thirty-five-year-old man who had just been fired from his job. He felt strongly that his job was his calling, so losing his job (his career) was the same to him as losing his calling. He felt "uncalled" and that he had lost his place in God's sight.

This man expressed his agonizing pain in words having to do with being out of God's will and being kicked out of God's kingdom. What he needed to know, and what I told him, was that his calling is indeed a kingdom calling, but that being called into God's kingdom is a matter of salvation, and his salvation is secure. That is a far cry from job security. He cannot lose his salvation—his calling—as he lost his job.

"I am free," he replied. "I am a Christian!" And I am free too, as I confidently apply in my own life the knowledge that the Lord of my life can lead me through any job changes that he desires—because I am his! *And as he does lead me* in that way, then I know for sure that I am truly free. That is what wholehearted integration is all about.

The example above answers very clearly one of our two opening questions: Is integration complete when it is only intellectual? The answer to the other question, however, is not quite so clear. Should theology be the guardian discipline for protecting the truth? It is fairly easy for some conceptual relation models to give theology that position in a counterproductive way. For others there is no need to give theology a superior position, so that it balances out. Therefore, although critical integration gives an affirmative answer to both questions, embodied integration gives a negative answer to both.

A combination of critical and embodied integration also gives a negative answer. Therefore, wholehearted integration would certainly say no to both questions.

Notes

1. Lyon, D. *Sociology and the human image.* Downers Grove, Ill.: Inter-Varsity, 1983, chaps. 1, 9.

2. Farnsworth, K. E. *Integrating psychology and theology: Elbows together but hearts apart.* Washington D. C.: University Press of America, 1981, chaps. 1–2.

3. Lyon, *Sociology and the human image,* pp. 31–34, 190–95.

4. Holmes, A. F. *Contours of a world view.* Grand Rapids: Wm. B. Eerdmans, 1983, chaps. 3–4.

5. Wolterstorff, N. *Reason within the bounds of religion.* Grand Rapids: Wm. B. Eerdmans, 1976.

6. Thorson, W. R. The biblical insights of Michael Polanyi. *Journal of the American Scientific Affliliation* 33 (1981): 129–38, quotation on p. 135.

7. Holmes, *Contours of a world view,* preface.

8. Donne, J. *Devotions upon emergent occasions.* Reprinted. Ann Arbor: University of Michigan, 1960, pp. 108–9.

9. Taylor J. V. *Enough is enough: A biblical call for moderation in a consumer-oriented society.* Minneapolis: Augsburg, 1977, pp. 40-45.

10. Lyon, *Sociology and the human image,* chap. 2.

11. Evans, C. S. *Preserving the person: A look at the human sciences.* Grand Rapids: Baker Book House, 1982, chap. 11.

12. Holmes, *Contours of a world view,* chap. 7.

13. Evans, *Preserving the person,* pp. 167–68.

14. Berkhof, H. *Christ and the powers,* trans. John H. Yoder. Scottdale, Pa.; Herald, 1977, p. 66.

15. Ibid., pp. 49–50.

16. Ibid., p. 52.

17. Wallach, M. A., and Wallach, L. *Psychology's sanction for selfishness: The error of egoism in theory and therapy.* San Francisco: W. H. Freeman, 1983, chaps. 1, 10.

18. Kilpatrick, W. K. *Psychological seduction: The failure of modern psychology.* New York: Thomas Nelson, 1983, chap. 3.

19. Ibid., p. 31.

20. Kohlberg, L. Moral stages and moralization: The cognitive-developmental approach. *In Moral development and behavior: Theory; research, and social issues,* ed. T. Lickona. New York: Holt, Rinehart and Winston, 1976, chap. 2.

21. Quoted in H. Muson. Moral thinking: Can it be taught? *Psychology Today* 12(9) (1979): 48–68, 92, quotation on p. 57.

22. Wolterstorff, N. *Educating for responsible action.* Grand Rapids: Wm. B. Eerdmans, 1980, chap. 8.

23. Evans, *Preserving the person,* p. 14.

24. Bandura, A. The self system in reciprocal determinism. *American Psychologist* 33, (1978), p. 350.

25. Van Leeuwen, M. S. *The sorcerer's apprentice: A Christian look at the changing face of psychology*. Downers Grove, Ill.: Inter-Varsity, 1982.

26. Cosgrove, M. P. *B. F. Skinner's behaviorism: An analysis*. Grand Rapids: Zondervan, 1982.

27. Jeeves, M. A. *Psychology and Christianity: The view both ways.* Downers Grove, Ill.: Inter-Varsity, 1976, chaps. 3, 6.

28. Myers, D. G. *The human puzzle: Psychological research and Christian belief.* San Francisco: Harper & Row, 1978; *The inflated self: Human illusions and the biblical call to hope*. New York: Seabury, 1981; Ludwig, T. E.; Westphal, M.; Klay, R. J.; and Myers, D. G. *Inflation, poortalk, and the Gospel;* Bolt, M., and Myers, D. G.; Valley Forge, Judson, 1981. *The human connection: How people change people.* Downers Grove, Ill.: Inter-Varsity, 1984. Solzhenitsyn, A. I. *A world split apart: Commencement address delivered at Harvard University, June 8, 1978,* trans. Irina Ilovayskaya Alberti. New York: Harper & Row, 1978, pp. 15–19.

29. The other world-view component is servanthood. See K. E. Farnsworth, Furthering the kingdom in psychology. In *The Making of a Christian Mind: A Christian World View & the academic enterprise,* ed. A. Holmes. Downers Grove, Ill.: Inter-Varsity, 1985, chap. 4.

30. I have developed the full scope of the problem of professionalism in K. E. Farnsworth. Christian psychotherapy and the culture of professionalism. *Journal of Psychology and Theology* 8 (1980): 115–21.

31. Ebersole, M. Conflict in clinical practice. Paper presented at the Eastern Area Mennonite Professionalism Conference, New York, February, 1979.

32. Reese, B. Within or outside the system: An Anabaptist perspective. Paper presented at the Eastern Area Mennonite Professionalism Conference, New York, February, 1979.

33. Larzelere, R. E. The task ahead: Six levels of integration of Christianity and psychology. *Journal of Psychology and Theology* 8 (1980): 3–11.

34. Farnsworth, K. E. The conduct of integration. *Journal of Psychology and Theology* 10 (1982): 308–19.

35. DeVries, M. J. Beyond integration: New directions. *The CAPS Bulletin* 7(3) (1981): 1–5, quotation on p. 3.

36. A Christian liberal arts college is potentially the best educational context for students to learn sound methodological and hermeneutical principles and procedures. Context, however, does not guarantee content: even though the pertinent courses are offered, it does not necessarily mean that the issues treated here will be covered.

37. Farnsworth, Conduct of integration, p. 317.

38. DeVries, Beyond integration, p. 3.

39. Carter, J. D. and Narramore, B. *The integration of psychology and theology: An introduction.* Grand Rapids: Zondervan, 1979, chaps. 4–7.

40. Collins, G. R. *Psychology and theology: Prospects for integration*. Nashville: Abingdon, 1981, chap. 1.

41. Van Leeuwen, *Sorcerer's apprentice,* chap. 3. This is the best presentation of Stephen Evans's models for actually relating psychology and Christianity.

42. Everett, W. W. and Bachmeyer, T. J. *Disciplines in transformation: A guide to theology and the behavioral sciences.* Washington, D. C.: University Press of America, 1979, chap. 9.

43. Niebuhr, H. R. *Christ and culture.* New York: Harper & Row, 1951, chaps. 2–6.

44. I am especially referring to the critiques in A. Dueck, and G. Zerbe, Interpretations

of Christ and culture: The church, the world and the profession, paper presented at the Christian Association for Psychological Studies Convention, Santa Barbara, June, 1976; and J. H. Yoder, "Christ and culture": A critique of H. Richard Niebuhr, unpublished paper, 1976.

45. Crabb, L. J., Jr. *Effective biblical counseling.* Grand Rapids: Zondervan, 1977.

46. Rokeach, M. *The open and closed mind.* New York: Basic Books, 1960, introduction.

47. Sargant, W. *Battle for the mind: A physiology of conversion and brain-washing.* London: William Heinemann, 1957.

48. This idea was suggested by R. S. Valle, and R. von Eckartsberg, eds., *The metaphors of consciousness.* New York: Plenum, 1981, p. 157.

49. Ellul, J. *Hope in time of abandonment.* New York: Seabury, 1973, p. 133

50. May, R. *Psychology and the human dilemma.* Princeton, N. J.: Van Nostrand, 1967, p. 219.

51. Koteskey, R. L. *Psychology from a Christian perspective.* Nashville: Abingdon, 1980, chap. 11.

52. Cosgrove, *B. F. Skinner's behaviorism.*

53. Fromm, E. *Man for himself.* New York: Holt, Rinehart, & Winston, 1947, chap. 3.

54. Oden, T. C. *The intensive group experience: The new pietism.* Philadelphia: Westminster, 1972, pp. 73–75.

55. Farnsworth, Conduct of integration, p. 317.

56. Bube, R. H. *The human quest: A new look at science and the Christian faith.* Waco: Word Books, 1971, p. 34.

57. MacKay, D. M. *The clockwork, image: A Christian perspective on science.* Downers Grove, Ill.: Inter-Varsity, 1974, p. 91.

58. Ibid., p. 37.

59. Jeeves, *Psychology and Christianity.*

60. Haas, J. W., Jr. Complementarity and Christian thought—An assessment: 2. Logical complementarity. *Journal of the American Scientific Affiliation* 35 (1983): 203–9; Orlebeke, C. J. Donald MacKay's philosophy of science. *Christian Scholar's Review* 7 (1977): 51–63.

61. Thorson, W. R. The spiritual dimensions of science. In *Horizons of science,* ed. C. H. F. Henry, chap. 11.

62. For further clarification, see A. D. Compaan, Biblical norms for career choice. *The CAPS Bulletin* 5(2) (1979): 12–17. I wish to acknowledge this article as the source of several of the ideas in this brief section on calling and making career decisions.

4

Truth, the Bible, and the Person

Integration of psychology and theology is based on three realities: the reality of truth, the reality of the Bible, and the reality of the person. In order to understand fully the nature of integration, we must therefore understand the nature of these three fundamental realities.

This final chapter will be an overview of the nature of truth, the Bible, and the person. These are the objects of the psychological and theological methods we have already discussed, as well as the integrative methods we have detailed. It is naturally assumed that the object of all the methods is truth. And the objects of theological and psychological study are, of course, the Bible and the person, respectively.

We will now see that fully knowing truth, which is what wholehearted integration is all about, is a matter of both intellectual understanding and commitment through action—talking with God plus walking with God. We will also see that the Bible and the person are related to God by their very nature, so that the truths that God reveals through each of them are accessible through dialogue with him. That is, through the disciplines of theology and psychology. In addition, we will consider two very important integration issues: Can one truth be truer than another? How does God reveal his truths through the biblical data studied by theologians as compared with the personal data studied by psychologists?

The Nature of Truth

We have already examined two approaches to integration—critical integration and embodied integration. Each has two stages, review and incorporation, and relation and application, respectively. Psychological findings can be reviewed from a Christian perspective and then incorporated into one's thinking, or psychological findings and theological findings can be related conceptually and then applied in one's everyday living. Now I would like to introduce an initial stage that is common to both approaches and precedes the first stage of each one. This is the stage of discovery.

Every conceivable approach to integration is based initially on the discovery of truths through the disciplines of psychology and theology. This is the methodological starting point. The problem with this preliminary discovery stage, however, is the tendency of many Christians to overly identify the truths that are discovered with the process of discovering those truths. Some believe that truths, especially biblical truths, are completely unambiguous and can be discovered through an interpretation process that is totally free of human contamination. Others believe that truths are by their very nature ambiguous and can only be approximated through a personally creative interpretive process.

The true nature of truth, however, is between the two extremes. I believe that the existence of truth and the process of knowing truth, rather than being cut from the same piece of cloth, are radically different. Together they are neither completely objective nor completely subjective. On the one hand, the existence of truth is metaphysically objective, or independent of any human person's knowledge of it as such. On the other, the process of knowing truth is epistemologically subjective, or dependent on human interpretation.

Arthur Holmes also divides the nature of truth into its metaphysical and epistemological aspects. Substituting "fact" for "truth," he states:

> Metaphysically, a fact is an objective state of affairs that pertains at a given time and place and in a given set of relationships, independently of whether any of us know it at all. Epistemologically, a fact is a "fact of experience," related to the whole complex flux of inner and outer experience of which it is a part. Subjectivity has intruded and shaped it. The facts we know, then, are not bare facts clothed only in a birthday suit of metaphysical objectivity, but "interprefacts" perceived and understood by a human person who clothes them in the habits of his human experience and perspective.[1]

Truth, then, as the human person knows it, is always a complex mixture of an independently objective truth (metaphysical objectivity) and an individual interpretation of it as truth (epistemological subjectivity).

From the discussion thus far it is readily apparent that the nature of truth is inseparable from the nature of knowing truth. What is involved in knowing truth?

Knowing Truth

Holmes again prescribes a division into the same two components: "Knowing [truth] is in every case an individual mix of subjective and objective factors."[2] It is therefore incumbent on us to reflect on how each of these factors enters into the process of knowing truth.

Consider the umpire in a baseball game. His job is to determine whether each pitch is a ball or a strike. In all likelihood, he will be one of three types. Umpire One will flatly declare, "I calls 'em the way they are!" More tenuously, Umpire Two "calls 'em the way I sees 'em." And Umpire Three will be emphatic that "they ain't nuttin' 'til I calls 'em!"

Umpire One illustrates the rationalist bias that knowing is a completely objective process, with unambiguous data being interpreted totally without subjectivity. Things just are. Umpire Three, on the other hand, illustrates the existentialist bias that knowing is a completely subjective process, with ambiguous data serving merely as a trigger for self-expressive interpretation. This is the Alice-in-Wonderland approach to knowing truth.

Umpires One and Three are the bad guys. Umpire Two is the good guy. He does not dichotomize the objective and subjective factors. In discerning truth it is not either/or—it is both/and. Certainly the umpire knows the pitch is for real; he has been struck by enough errant throws to know that. But he also has been involved in enough "rhubarbs" with disgruntled batters to know there are a variety of ways to call any particular pitch. He is an expert on metaphysical objectivity and epistemological subjectivity. Let us, now, take a closer look at these two components of the knowing process.

Objectivity

Objectivity is a defining characteristic of both the existence of truth and the process of knowing truth. In addition to the truth being independent of human knowledge of it as such, knowing it is dependent on contact with reality other than one's own imagination. However, contact brings subjectivity into the equation.

Objectivity and subjectivity together constitute human knowing. This means that the distinctives of a particular truth must be brought into human consciousness, which can only be done through interaction. The human knower must dialogue with those distinctives on their own terms so they can tell their own story, yet in a way that the knower can understand them. Knowing truth cannot be an objective process without this kind of interaction between the distinctive features (object qualities) of the truth and the individual way of knowing of the knower. In short, human knowing is not objective if there is no personal interaction with the truths to be known.

The apostle Thomas is an excellent example. He demanded objectivity by asking to actually touch the resurrected Jesus. This is what Thomas needed in order to grasp the truth that the Jesus who died (the historical Jesus) was the same one who arose (the messianic Christ). We have no more objective witness than that, and it was due equally to the objectivity of the resurrected Christ and the subjectivity of doubting Thomas. As a believer who appreciates truly objective evidence, and as a psychologist who values truly objective data, I am grateful for Thomas's way of knowing truth.

Objective knowledge is experiential knowledge, according to eminent psychologist Abraham Maslow, not spectator knowledge.[3] It is based on involvement, not detachment. Sigmund Koch also points out that it is based on meaningful thinking, not ameaningful thinking.[4] In his discussion of the pathology of knowledge, Koch describes ameaningful thinking as a form of "epistemopathy" that regards its object as physically distant and faceless and reduces the knowing process to nothing more than gimmickry.

> *Ameaningful* thought or inquiry regards knowledge as the result of "processing" rather than discovery. It presumes that knowledge is an almost automatic result of a gimmickry, an assembly line, a "methodology." It assumes that inquiring action is so rigidly and fully regulated by rule that in its conception of inquiry it often allows the rules totally to displace their human users. . . . The terms and relations of the object of inquiry or the problem are seen, as it were, through an inverted telescope: Detail, structure, quiddity, are obliterated. Objects of knowledge become caricatures, if not faceless, and thus they lose reality.[5]

Such inquiry loses its objectivity.

> On the other hand, *meaningful* thinking involves a direct perception of unveiled, vivid relations that seem to spring from the quiddities, particularities, of the objects of thought, the problem situations that form the occasions of thought. There is an organic determination of the form and substance of thought by the properties of the object and the terms of the problem. In meaningful thinking, the mind caresses, flows joyously into, over, around, the relational matrix defined by the problem, the object. There is a merging of person and object or problem.[6]

That is objectivity.

Subjectivity

It is possible, of course, to become too involved with the object or the problem and lose objectivity by being too subjective. But this is not a problem of subjectivity, it is a problem of subjectivism.

Subjectivism is an actual loss of contact with the object of inquiry from over-attention to one's own feelings, thoughts, or whatever. It is a situation in which I cannot see your tears because I cannot see through my own. This sort of over-involvement is probably what has given subjectivity a bad name. We should not, however, throw the baby out with the bath water.

Subjectivity is the degree of involvement with the object of inquiry that allows for personal interpretation while maintaining fidelity to the objective qualities of the object itself. A large factor in any such interpretation is the personality of the knower, which has been demonstrated repeatedly throughout history. Biologist Stephen Jay Gould, for example, has documented several situations that clearly reveal science to be a "gutsy, human enterprise," a "socially embedded activity [that] progresses by hunch, vision, and intuition."[7] In fact, he concludes that the most creative theories are not the result of inexorable induction from pure, unsullied facts at all. Rather, both the facts and the theories they support often result from the intrusion of human personality: facts from a priori prejudice that distorts the data-gathering process, and theories from imaginative visions being further imposed upon those facts.

Of course the intrusion of human personality into the knowing process can have negative effects, which Gould chronicles with a passion. Among his findings, for instance, is the discovery that H. H. Goddard (who invented the word "moron") actually altered photographs to fit his prejudice that the Kallikak (a name he also invented) family living in poverty in New Jersey was mentally retarded. Others have similarly reanalyzed the works of Sigmund Freud, Jean Piaget, and Margaret Mead and noted the negative effects of personal bias.[8] In the latter's case, it is concluded that her "discoveries" regarding Samoan life that contributed so heavily to the sexual revolution in the middle of this century were nothing more than the imposition of her own beliefs onto the evidence.

It must also be noted that human personality affects the knowing process, not only through thinking, but through feelings as well. This is undoubtedly a familiar point by now, since I have already discussed the synonymous terms "intentionality," "nonrationality," and the preconceptual component of world-view thinking. Feelings are the same thing.

The importance of the nonrational, or preconceptual, aspects of human experience is not always appreciated, however. Indeed, B. F. Skinner "translates" feelings into introspective observations of inner physical states that are associated with behaving in certain ways but that do not in any way initiate or direct behavior. Feelings are the passive result of behavior—including thinking, which Skinner defines as verbal behavior—and therefore do not directly affect the knowing process.[9]

Others do not agree. Maurice Merleau-Ponty, for example, argued for the *primacy* of perceptual, preconceptual experience. For him, preconceptual sensing was the foundation for—not the result of—conceptual thinking.[10] For Freud too, perceptual processes were the bottom line for the cognitive ego functions, and of course he made a strong case for the power of unconscious motivation.

More recently, psychologist R. B. Zajonc has picked up the argument for the primacy of affect, or feeling.[11] He reasons convincingly that the various forms of preconceptual experience that can be collectively referred to as feelings derive from a separate and partly independent system in the organism. With the backing of research findings, he concludes that separate neuroanatomical structures can in fact be identified for feelings and cognition (thinking) and that feelings frequently precede and at times are quite independent of cognitive activity.

It would seem, based on Zajonc's evidence, that feelings most certainly do directly affect the knowing process. Knowing truth is directly affected by both preconceptual sensing and conceptual thinking. Such is the testimony of none other than Albert Einstein, who once described his pursuit of truth as a progression from the preconceptual to the conceptual.

> (A) The words or the language, as they are written or spoken, do not seem to play any role in my mechanism of thought. The

psychical entities which seem to serve as elements in thought are certain signs and more or less clear images which can be "voluntarily" reproduced and combined.

There is, of course, a certain connection between those elements and relevant logical concepts. It is also clear that the desire to arrive finally at logically connected concepts is the emotional basis of this rather vague play with the above mentioned elements. But taken from a psychological viewpoint, this combinatory play seems to be the essential feature in productive thought—before there is any connection with logical construction in words or other kinds of signs which can be communicated to others.

(B) The above mentioned elements are, in my case, of visual and some of muscular type. Conventional words or other signs have to be sought for laboriously only in a secondary stage, when the mentioned associative play is sufficiently established and can be reproduced at will.[12]

This preconceptual-conceptual progression in knowing truth has also been described most eloquently in a Christian context.

Even when the Word of God strikes a man without warning, when there is a sudden conversion, an inner call, which changes all at once the direction of his life, he perceives that God has been speaking to him for a long time, that the dialogue was already going on in the darkness of the unconscious before it broke out into the full light of day.[13]

Throughout this book an important theme has been that subjectivity and objectivity, in one form or another, complete each other. They are, in Rudolf Otto's words, "the warp and woof of the complete fabric." In discovering truth, one has a subjective encounter with an objective reality. The encounter is made up of both feeling and thinking, and both are meaningful in and of themselves. The former, however, must be progressively charged with significance from the latter.

Our integrative efforts depend on keeping the balance in our search for psychological and theological truths. An *im*balance usually occurs when we forget that our search for truth needs to be excitable as well as reasonable and sensitive as well as sensible.

When that happens, our search for truth is all in our heads, we become top-heavy, and integration falls flat on its face. In addition, we are apt to believe that we not only know the truth but that now we also have the truth.

Having Truth

When we try to eliminate subjectivity from the discovery stage of integration, by coming up with truths that are uncontaminated by feelings, we fall right back into the trap of rationalistic bias. We get all hung up on methodological purity and epistemological certainty. In other words, we believe that because of our totally objective method of knowing, we can know truth with absolute certainty—we can own it.

Of course we realize by now that knowing truth is always a mixture of subjective and objective factors. Therefore I would prefer to talk about certitude, rather than certainty. The difference is one of degree; conviction rather than dogmatism. It is also one of direction; justification rather than proof. The direction of one's search for truth should be toward justifying one's faith in the absoluteness of God's truth, rather than toward proving with absolute certainty that one knows God's truth. "To prove a belief indisputably true may be asking too much of human knowing, but to justify believing it true is not."[14]

Knowing truth with the confidence and conviction of certitude gives me enough epistemological humility to further realize that I do not have the truth, but rather the truth has me. Truth has demand-character. It calls me into question, not the other way around.

Truth demands a response. It is dynamic, not inert. Truth does not just lie there, like oatmeal in a bowl. It is like a crooked picture on the wall that begs to be straightened, or the musical progression that calls for completion.[15] "Truth is a snare: you cannot have it, without being caught. You cannot have the truth in such a way that you catch it, but only in such a way that it catches you."[16]

Truth exists, then, in spite of me but not for me, unless I respond to it and appropriate it into my own life. This step of commitment, or application, is what completes both the process of knowing a particular truth and the process of integrating it. At this stage they become one and the same. From discovery to application, it is a process of intellectual understanding plus commitment through action, or simply talking with God and walking with God.

Personal commitment is the key. It is by *following* Jesus that I know the truth, and the truth has me. This is how my knowledge of Jesus becomes truly objective. Canadian chemist and lay theologian Walter Thorson concludes the same thing.

> "P is true" is really functionally equivalent to the statement "I believe P," and there is not the slightest additional "proof" I can bring to show that "P" *is* true, apart from the responsible thoughts, words, choices, and actions consistent with "I believe P"—and which, *presumably,* I am already engaged in, in manifesting the reality of which "P" speaks. That is the limit of my creaturely powers and responsibilities.
>
> Such a conclusion is not a despairing proclamation of "the final subjectivity of all claims to know." On the contrary, it is the affirmation that a knowledge which is personal can nevertheless be objective. When we are forced to recognize that all the knowledge we possess, even of the most incontrovertible objective realities, involves our personal participation in responsible commitment, then it is absurd to conclude that objectivity [sic] knowledge cannot exist: the proper conclusion is the opposite one, i.e., that "objectivity" is not the removal of personal involvement but its *responsible exercise.*[17]

We must come to the conclusion that the result of completing the process of knowing truth (or of wholeheartedly integrating truth) by living it in our daily lives is the single best testimony we can give as to its veracity. We may also, because of this, however, begin to have more confidence in one truth than in another. But that in no way means one truth is *truer* than the other.

For those who include personal commitment as the finishing step in knowing truth, then, there is no cause to set some truths up as "truer" than others. They are either true, or they are false. By shifting our focus from the truth per se to the person knowing the truth, we can see that it is really a matter of clarity of vision and degree of confidence. Those who attempt to exclude subjectivity altogether from the knowing process (which is impossible) are incorrect in their claim to "possess" truer truths than those known by other than "purely" formal, rational means. Because of the inevitability of epistemological subjectivity, all actual truths are ultimately known in the same way. Therefore, we must finally conclude, in answer to the first question asked at the beginning of this chapter, that one truth can definitely not be truer than another.

The Nature of the Bible

The fact that the Bible is the clearest source of our knowledge of truth does not eliminate the possibility of a whole host of epistemological problems, "nor does it impart a special status of rational certainty to our knowledge itself. We walk by faith: the truth is divine, but it is held by earthen vessels, human and fallible."[18] Having considered the nature of truth, which is both divine and held by human beings, we will be turning shortly to the nature of the person, who certainly is among other things, fallible.

But first, let us consider the nature of "the clearest source of our knowledge of truth," the Bible. This is the natural thing to do for two reasons. First, as "reservoir and conduit of divine truth,"[19] the Bible is positioned squarely between the divine and the human and is therefore a necessary link between the two. Second, it is just as important to understand the nature of the primary object of theological study—the Bible—as it is to understand human nature (the human person being the primary object of psychological study), if we hope to thoroughly understand the nature of integration.

The Dual Nature of Scripture

The Bible is a conduit between the divine and the human, which would indicate that it contains elements of both. Yet its name is the Holy Bible, which would seem to eliminate the human side of its nature. This suggests the first issue concerning Scripture.

Does an emphasis on the human nature of the Bible detract from its divine nature?

It is easy to understand why many Christians resist the dual-nature concept of Scripture. They fear, and rightly so, that Scripture's divinity can too easily be overshadowed and in some cases even denied. Once one begins to reflect on the nature of an authority such as the Bible, the questioning can gain momentum and end in total "humanization" or rejection of any divine authority whatsoever.

Nevertheless, Scripture was originally written in human language and is accessible to modern-day cultures through a variety of human translations into their particular languages. In addition, each reading of Scripture is a further human interpretation of a biblical author's intended meaning. Any consideration of the nature of the Bible must recognize the human participation at every level of its existence, in spite of any excesses that might conceivably result.

Affirmation of the human character of Scripture does not in any way necessitate a diluting of its holy character. The divine inspiration of Scripture does not have to be called into question. Rather, an improvement in the human interpretation of Scripture will more than likely be the result. God has spoken to us through the testimony of human witnesses, who received his revelation and recorded it. And, according to G. C. Berkouwer, the dean of scholarly evangelical theologians, it is only through our acknowledgment of this verbal humanness of the Bible that we can "do full justice to the rich variation of the biblical witness that speaks of law and gospel, of promise and fulfillment, and that reechoes God's voice to us through all the tensions of human life."[20]

Once the dual-nature concept of Scripture has been accepted, it is quite easy to draw parallels with Christ's dual nature. Berkouwer points out that the analogy between "inscripturation" and incarnation, against the background that the Word became flesh, can lead to greater insight into numerous difficult questions concerning Scripture. He warns us, however, not to take the analogy too literally, and gives several reasons why.[21] All things considered, the analogy is helpful in at least the two following areas.

The Docetic View of Scripture

When the parallels between Scripture and Christ are fully developed, they prevent a docetic view of either. "Docetism" was the name given to the practice of those in the early church who tried to minimize the significance of Christ's humanity. It also applied to the doctrine of Scripture that minimized the human character of Scripture in order to defend against any number of heresies. But as the church grew in its christological and scriptural understanding, the human and divine aspects of both came more clearly into focus. Consequently, Berkouwer can proclaim today:

> We may not risk tarnishing the mystery of Scripture by disqualifying the God-ordained way in which it came to us. Moreover, to think that the trustworthiness of Scripture is protected by means of a docetic view of it is to display a totally wrong concept of Scripture. Amidst many dangers, the conviction has gradually become stronger that the human character of Scripture is not an accidental or peripheral condition of the Word of God but something that legitimately deserves our full attention.[22]

The Servant-Form of Scripture

The fully developed analogy between inscripturation and incarnation not only keeps us from a view of Scripture that tarnishes its nature, but also helps us develop a view of Scripture consistent with "the God-ordained way in which it came to us."

Probably the most consistent view is one that considers Scripture to be in the form of a servant. Berkouwer, agreeing, does not feel that this in any way diminishes Scripture's authority and normativity. The most obvious reason is that Jesus himself took on the form of a servant. He came to serve, not to be served. He emptied himself and humbled himself—he was a suffering servant. And yet he retained his exaltedness and his authority. Likewise, Scripture came into being to "be of service to the speaking of God."[23] Scripture too took a human form—of word and writing—and thereby became subject to the uneven fate of all human writing. Yet Scripture also, because of its divine nature, retains its own exalted status and does not cease speaking with authority.

So the view that God's Word in human writing is in servant form is a good one. In the form of a servant, Scripture is under the lordship of and in the service of the Lord of all creation. This gives it an aura of consecration and power. At the same time, Scripture in the form of a servant is part of the human creation, with all the weaknesses and limitations attributable to human words. This reveals its vulnerability to misrepresentation and misinterpretation. The parallels with Christ, the greatest servant, are very close, and it is because inscripturation and incarnation appear to be cut from the same cloth that I believe the servant-view of Scripture is a correct view.

Prominent evangelical theologian Bernard Ramm, following the thinking of Martin Luther, also believes that our doctrine of Scripture must be of the same heartbeat as our theology of God's other revelation events—most particularly the event of the cross.

> God's written Word is in the form of humiliation just as the Son of God in his incarnation. It too shares the brokenness, the servanthood, the masking of the divine glory as the incarnate Son. . . . Yahweh of the Old Testament leads a hidden, mysterious existence, for he alone will be worshipped and adored. And we dare not have a version of Scripture that betrays the nature in which Yahweh encounters man.[24]

In other words, the servant-form of Scripture is entirely consistent with the ordained way in which God has always encountered men and women throughout history. And it is consistent with the biblical witness giving testimony to the lordship of its Creator, rather than to itself. Anything less would betray the whole revelatory process.

It is safe to conclude, with Berkouwer, that "the form of a servant does not [humanize] revelation but passes it on and reveals its true riches."[25]

The Authority of Scripture

A second issue worthy of consideration concerns the authority of Scripture, and there have been some real battles fought over this one. On the one hand, there are those who want to have a clear doctrinal statement about the Bible's authority in order to prevent any erosion of the place of Scripture at the center of one's faith and practice. On the other hand, there are those who do not want any such statement to become a guarantee of the centrality of Scripture in people's lives to the exclusion of God himself. In other words, they do not allow commitment to doctrinal purity to elevate human power to a place where the lordship of the Creator over the biblical witness can be ignored.

I hasten to point out that it is entirely appropriate for those who have come into relationship with their Creator through the biblical witness, and who continue to fellowship with him through the biblical witness, to give testimony to the authority of Scripture in their lives. Further, it is understandable that such testimony would have a definite air of certainty and take the form of unequivocal doctrinal statements that would be affirmed by countless other believers. But what about the unbeliever? How does this person come initially to believe in scriptural authority? Does it come from exposure to doctrinal statements that have arisen from the long-standing experience and as an expression of the high degree of certitude of those who already believe?

We will consider two sides of the issue. First, what is deeply ingrained certitude regarding the authority of Scripture based on? Second, what is initial belief in the authority of Scripture based on?

Certitude

In the Augustinian tradition of faith seeking understanding, G. C. Berkouwer clearly rejects the notion that an a priori theory or postulate is necessary as the basis for certitude regarding the authority of Scripture. Therefore, he would undoubtedly agree that a person with a high degree of certitude and strong commitment to a corresponding doctrinal statement probably did not achieve the former because of the latter. Certitude "is not and cannot be based on a theoretical reflection on what, according to our insight, must be the nature of the divine revelation and on which ways and forms it must have come to us in order to be the guarantee of certainty."[26] The way to certitude is through subjection to the Scripture itself.

> The repeated doxology on the words of the Lord as being pure words, purified seven times (Ps. 12:6), as truth (Ps. 119:160), as righteous (Ps. 119:144), as a lamp and light (Ps. 119:105), and as a joy of the heart, simply cannot be the result of a postulate nor guaranteed by one. They can be sung only in faith, experience, and heartfelt love (Ps. 119:111, 113). The trustworthiness of the Word does not subject itself to an *a priori* testing, but can only be understood in the all-pervasive power of the Word itself as the sword of the Spirit. . . . The way to certainty and faith in Scripture is the way of which Jeremiah in his encounter with God testifies: "O Lord, thou hast deceived me, and I was deceived; thou art stronger than I, and thou hast prevailed" (Jer. 20:7).[27]

"The way is pointed out to us," Berkouwer says, and "only by walking this way can we confess that Holy Scripture is the Word of God." He goes on to say, however, that this does *not* mean that "Scripture . . . *becomes* God's Word 'through its use.'"[28] Thus, he takes a definite stand on the hotly contested issue over whether the Bible is truly God's Word independent of its use or becomes so only when used. The most that can be said is that the Bible is truly understood as God's Word only as I use it; certainly no theory about the Bible being God's Word could convince me as deeply. But that in no way speaks to the reality of the Bible as God's Word in spite of me (whether I read it or not). At most, then, "its use" is important only in establishing the Bible as God's Word *for me* but not *in spite of me*.

Berkouwer summarizes this aspect of the nature of the Bible:

> In the case of [Scripture] *becoming* God's Word, a sort of transubstantiation would take place, occurring in "its use." If one understands the significance of God's word in the human words of Scripture, he will quickly reject this dilemma as completely fruitless. For it is incorrect and offers no true perspective on the God-breathed Scripture.
>
> The debate about the question "before and apart from its use" or "in its use" is meaningful only insofar as it deals with the interest in the priority and sovereignty of the Scripture that confronts us with its witness. It does not and cannot derive its authority from the fact that *we* use it, not even when we use Scripture in faith. For

> because of its nature and origin the witness of Scripture evokes its use as real testimony. The message of the God-breathed Scripture, which comes "from beyond us" and is meant "for us," becomes clear precisely through the correct use of Scripture while hearing and understanding it. While all subjectivism regarding Scripture is being rejected, it must also be taken into account that Scripture can be known only together with its purpose—implying both its use and application.[29]

Belief

It is very easy for high-certitude, doctrinally committed believers, because of the depth of their conviction, to expect unbelievers to begin the journey of faith by first accepting the obvious: the Bible is in fact the Word of God and can be totally trusted as authoritative. While this may be the unqualified conclusion of believers regarding the Bible, we have just seen that they probably did not arrive at such a position of certitude by *subscribing* to a doctrinal statement *about* the Bible but rather by *submerging* themselves *in* the Bible itself. Keeping that in mind the question is, Where should one encourage the unbeliever to begin?

Should the point of departure be a preceding guarantee about the authority of the Bible, before actual interaction with the Bible itself? Or should the unbeliever get involved right from the start with the biblical witness and thereby experience its authority directly, without being sidetracked by intellectual discussions about its authority?

Theology professor Paul Holmer warns of the clear danger of the first approach.

> Instead of learning who God is and how to live in his accord, one learns a lot of things . . . about the book. If it is the word of God, then one should learn with it, for it is a lamp to our feet, a light in the darkened world, by which to find one's way. But strangely enough, theories about dispensations, inspiration, authorship, and a lot else, begin to intervene. It almost looks as if a chief piece of theology . . . has to be made up . . . to get the business moving. And soon the fireworks are not in the gospels and the epistles but in the . . . scheme about the book.[30]

Belief in the authority of Scripture is based on nothing more than "a system of warrants, a passel of guarantees"[31] that detract from the real business of "learning who God is and how to live in his accord."

When the focus shifts from the Author to the Book, it is easy to forget that the purpose of the biblical witness is to point to God, not to draw attention to itself. In the extreme, such a shift in emphasis can become a form of idolatry—"bibliolatry"—where the Bible itself is worshiped as the living Word. Balance needs to be restored. "The Bible is indeed God's Word Written, and it most infallibly contains all things necessary for salvation. But it is also a thing. It is not the Mystery."[32]

The hymn writer had the correct balance, when she wrote:

> O send Thy Spirit, Lord,
> Now unto me,
> That He may touch my eyes
> And make me see:
> Show me the truth concealed
> Within Thy Word,
> And in Thy book revealed
> I see the Lord.[33]

This is the only real basis for both initial belief in and deeply ingrained certitude regarding the authority of Scripture. And, it is totally consistent with the servant-form of Scripture and the dual nature of Scripture.

By now it has become apparent that the human element is critical for our continued discussion. It is absolutely essential in any attempt to understand the nature of truth and the nature of the Bible, as well as all the other component parts of the integration process. Let us now take a look at the nature of the human element itself.

The Nature of the Person

Earlier I mentioned that truth is held by earthen vessels, human and fallible. Fallibility is indeed one of the chief characteristics of human nature. Human imperfections are obvious for everyone to see. And fallible vessels that we are, it is easy to acknowledge another characteristic of human nature, our creatureliness.

An awareness of our creatureliness can prevent us from adopting the "horticultural view of self" that is quite common in some psychological and educational circles today. This is, again, the view that assumes a person is filled with goodness that must be allowed to just ooze forth—like a rose unfolding from a rosebud—unburdened by any sort of limitation. Such a view assumes no sin in human nature.

Awareness of our creatureliness also shows us that we are dependent by nature on God and all of his creation. It is the kind of dependence that is best expressed by the Hebrew word *shalom:* harmony with all creation, informed at every point by answerability to God.[34] In other words, we are relational beings. We must live in harmonious relationship with God, others, and the world around us if we are to be nourished and fulfilled as human beings.

Relatedness is a third primary characteristic of human nature, which by no means completes the list of the most important characteristics. It is, however, the one we will elaborate at some length here. In doing so, we will focus attention on the most important of all human relationships, the human-divine.

Relationship with God

> What were we made for? To know God. What aim should we set ourselves in life? To know God. What is the "eternal life" that Jesus gives? Knowledge of God. . . . What is the best thing in life, bringing more joy, delight, and contentment, than anything else? Knowledge of God.[35]
>
> I do not myself believe that the Christian ever, in this life, passes for good and all out of the one cry into the other, out of Romans 7 into Romans 8, out of despair into victory. No. He is always crying for deliverance, and he is always exulting in his Deliverer.[36]

Whether through the joy and contentment of victory or through deliverance from despair, our knowledge of—relationship with—God is what makes the difference.

But what, in terms of the nature of the person, makes relationship with God possible? We can look at this question in two ways. We are created in God's image, and we are created with the capacity to be indwelled by God in the form of the Holy Spirit. Then, expanding the time-frame of the question, we will consider the issue of whether we are created with an immortal soul or are re-created for eternal fellowship with God.

Image of God

The most basic reason for our relation to God is our similarity with him. We are created in his image. What, then, does being created in the image of God mean?

First, what it does not mean is described in an amazing interpretation of the creation account in the book of Genesis:

> At the climax of the Creation process, God is represented as saying, "Let us make Man in our image." Why the plural? Who is the "us," the "our" of which God speaks? My suggestion for understanding that sentence is to see it as connected to the sentence immediately before it, in which God creates animals. . . . Having [first] created the animals and beasts, He says *to them:* "Let us arrange for a new kind of creature to emerge, a human being, in *our* image, yours and Mine. . . . You animals will contribute his physical dimension, and I will breathe a soul into him." And so, as the crown of Creation, human beings are created, part animal, part divine.[37]

Fortunately, it is a pretty rare type of exegetical excess that can come up with the conclusion that God and the animals are the "Us" and the "Our" in the statement, as it appears in Scripture, "Let Us make man in Our image"—note the difference in capitalization from the statement as it appears in the quote above.

The conclusion that humans are part animal and part divine, however, is quite common. Depending on the "part" being emphasized, the human person is often thought of as either a higher animal or a fallen god. Neither characterization, though, seems to represent adequately the truly unique nature of the person.[38] I do not believe the key is in "substance"—i.e., an animal "part" or a divine "part," either one alone or the two in combination. I believe instead that the key lies in the human capacity to be like God.

The emphasis should be less on "having" the image of God (as a substance) and more on *imaging* God (as a process). Imaging means being like. Scripture, in fact, advises us to imitate God: love as God loves, forgive as God forgives, and be merciful as God is merciful. It is this human capacity to imitate or be like God that represents the similarity with God that basically makes relationship with him possible.

Unfortunately there is a problem. The problem is the Fall. Everyone knows we do not relate perfectly with God. That is because our capacity to imitate or image God was damaged by the Fall. What we got was a capacity to sin as well. Everyone knows about that, too. But it is not at all obvious how these two capacities manage to persist generation after generation. Is it a matter of biological inheritance, or is something else involved?

I would like to suggest that the answer is more relational than biological. It is entirely possible that what we inherited from Adam was a broken relationship with God. And it is because of being born into this broken relationship (out of relationship) that sin enters our lives.

One implication is that we should talk about the nature of the person in a descriptive sense rather than a causal sense. For example, it is our nature to sin—i.e., we are sinners. Our nature does not "make" us sin. Nor do we have an inborn tendency to seek God, so that we initiate the relationship. Rather, God is the initiator and we respond. Biologically, each new generation is capable of responding, but individual relationships are continuously established with God throughout history because God himself chooses to act in history and initiate such relationships.

Another implication would be that although our capacity for imaging God has been marred from birth and continues to be remarred as an effect of sinning throughout life, it can be renewed and transformed. It is not set biologically. The apostle Paul seems to indicate as much in 2 Corinthians 3:18 and Colossians 3:10. So in spite of our sin-capacity, our imaging-capacity can prevail. This is what assures the continuing reality of relationship with God, but that is only half of the story.

Indwelling of the Holy Spirit

The other half of the story of human-divine relationship is the human capacity to be filled with, or indwelled by, God the Holy Spirit. Indwelling is, in fact, the main ingredient in the life of the Christian, who has responded through faith in Jesus Christ to the relationship-initiating activity of the Holy Spirit. Although it is universally understood that indwelling is *what* happens in the life of the Christian, it is not at all clear *how* it happens. How, then, does the Holy Spirit indwell the Christian person?

Indwelling, like imaging, is an activity that cannot be precisely demonstrated one way or another. However, I suggest that indwelling is a matter of breath, not blood. The Holy Spirit indwells through relationship, not residence (at least not in the literal sense). C. S. Lewis orients our thinking along these lines.

> There is nothing more in a regenerate man than in an unregenerate man, just as there is nothing more in a man who is walking in the right direction than in one who is walking in the wrong direction. In another sense, however, it might be said that the regenerate man is *totally* different from the unregenerate, for the regenerate life, the Christ that is formed in him, transforms every part of him.[39]

I am suggesting that Christ is "formed in" a person as that person images God, and that there truly is "nothing more" in the person. The metaphor of breath is the fitting one to convey the idea that the Holy Spirit indwells through relationship. We can picture the relationship "not like the blood that circulates in you but like the air in which you breathe."[40] Indwelling is like the inspiration of air—the Breath of God—which is so beautifully described by one of our great hymns.

> Breathe on me, Breath of God,
> Fill me with life anew,
> That I may love what Thou dost love
> And do what Thou wouldst do.
>
> Breathe on me, Breath of God,
> Until my heart is pure,
> Until with Thee I will one will—
> To do and to endure.[41]

There does not have to be a God-entity that resides inside a person for that person to interact with God. It is understandable, however, that those who wish to emphasize the centrality of the Holy Spirit's activity in the Christian's life might think of indwelling in just that way. In what more definite way could one emphasize the centrality of indwelling than to say the Holy Spirit is literally in the person?

What word other than "indwelling," whichever way it is defined, could more powerfully communicate the concrete and total effect of the Holy Spirit in the Christian's life? The reality of indwelling, however, is in the extent of the influence God actually has on a person, and this does not depend on a divine entity taking up residence within the person to ensure such influence. Rather, the power of God to affect a person's life is dependent upon the intensity of that person's relationship with him.

It is like using a hammer or a saw. When one is vigorously hammering or sawing away, engrossed in making something, the tool is actually an extension of the self—so much so that one says *I* am hammering or sawing. It is in the same sense that I dwell in the hammer or saw when I use it that God dwells in me when he uses me for his own good purpose—making something of me.

The possibility that indwelling is being "in relationship" rather than "in" is consistent with the Greek word for the Holy Spirit, *Paracletos*. The meaning of the word is, "One called alongside to help." So perhaps the most accurate thing to say is that the Holy Spirit resides "alongside" rather than "in" the Christian—which is just as good for communicating the concreteness and totality of the Holy Spirit's influence in the Christian's life.[42]

With the Holy Spirit alongside to help the Christian image God through relationship with him, the story is complete. But there is an addendum.

Immortality of the Soul

What about relationship with God in eternity? Is there anything about the nature of the person that makes such a relationship possible?

The human bridge to eternity is commonly considered to be the soul. Persons are assumed to have entities called souls that survive death for an eternity of fire or an eternity of fellowship with God. Non-Christians' immortal souls go to hell, the Christians' immortal souls go to heaven. There are at least two problems, however, with this scenario.

The first problem concerns soul as an entity. The Bible describes personhood as a unity—as a whole, not a collection of entities or parts. Even God the Father, Son, and Holy Spirit is described as a triunity—as three in one, as the triune God. Biblical terms describing dimensions of the human person, like mind, will, soul, and spirit, refer generally, although not always specifically, to the whole person seen from a particular angle. Each term, then, can be used as a representation of the person as a whole, each in its own special way.

It is helpful to note that the use of these terms in the Old and New Testaments is not very consistent. It is true that the Hebraic language of the Old Testament brings out the representational quality of the terms, while the Hellenistic language of the New Testament focuses more on each term in and of itself. The overall intent of the latter, however, seems to be emphasis rather than division and compartmentalization of the person.

For example, "mind" might be mentioned to emphasize the importance of one's thought-life, but "the being of man is a united whole and his reflective or cognitive faculties are never isolated from his total being."[43] Also, with reference to "will," it is evident that Scripture depicts man "as an agent with responsibility for his acts, rather than denoting a discrete faculty, 'the will,' and . . . that it is accordingly *the man* who chooses or desires or refuses, rather than 'his will.'"[44]

Similarly, "spirit" can be seen as a whole-person concept.

> The spirit of man . . . [is neither an] entity from some other world, seeking release to that other world, nor a synthesis that swallows up and blurs all distinctions. Rather, human spirit is a realized unity of the whole man that preserves, indeed is even posited on the grounds of, a continuing presence and operation of the bodily and soulish dimensions of the human self. . . .
>
> Man qua man, then, is a realized indissolvable unity of body and soul, denoted by the term "spirit," or, in contemporary language, "self" or "person."[45]

The basic distinction in the use of the terms "mind," "will," and "spirit" is between having and being—i.e., I do not *have* a spirit, I *am* spirit in the sense just described. The same holds true for "soul." According to Arthur Holmes, "'soul' (OT *nephesh,* NT *psychē*) is used of a living being, not of an immaterial, eternal entity imprisoned in a body, despite the fact that we have a destiny beyond death."[46] Soul, then, can be thought of as a "patterned interaction of living matter,"[47] the vitality of a living organism or the personality of a living being.

This brings us to the second problem, which concerns soul as immortal. Although immortality of the soul is no more provable than the alternatives regarding indwelling of the Holy Spirit or imaging God, I wish to assert that persons do not have immortal souls. This provides ground from which to answer the question Is there anything about the nature of the person that makes relationship with God in eternity possible? The answer I suggest is no.

The idea of an immortal soul did not originate in the Bible. David Myers chronicles its long history, from the Greek pagan religion of the sixth century, B.C., through Plato, to today.[48] He then cites theologian Oscar Cullmann's dramatization of the vivid contrast between Greek dualism and Christian holism as seen in Socrates' and Jesus' radically different approaches to death. Socrates discoursed serenely with his disciples on the day of his death and then, with sublime calm, drank the hemlock. For him, death was welcome. He would not die, for his soul would live on, so he believed. Jesus, on the other hand, a few hours before his death trembled and wept with his disciples. And then, as he hung from the cross, he cried out in anguish, "My God, my God, why hast thou forsaken me?" Jesus knew that death was total. Myers concludes:

> Unlike the Platonists, Christians do not believe that the divine attribute of immortality is intrinsic to human nature. But Christianity is not without its hope. It asserts that our lives possess value and hope, not because this is merited by our nature, but because God loves us. Christians believe that God values the lives he has created and that he will recreate them for eternity, *giving* us . . . what we do not otherwise have—immortality. This resurrection hope is not something less than immortality of the soul, it is something more—

> the reconstitution of the whole person without imperfection. It is a hope grounded in God's initiative, not in our natural state.[49]

So after all is said and done, our hope is in Jesus' resurrection and our own re-creation, not in the immortality of our souls. Jesus was the first to conquer death, when he rose in total from total death. No "soul" accomplished that before him or has done so since.

Our hope is not in immortality (part of the person does not die but lives on) but life after death (the whole person dies and is recreated after death). This may be a hard shift in thinking for some people because of the natural desire for a guarantee of life in eternity: a provision for continuity between one's earthly relationship with God and one's heavenly relationship with him. Reification of the soul would seem to be just perfect. Donald MacKay, however, gives us a better alternative—the memory of God.[50] For MacKay, the quality of our earthly life is preserved in the memory of God and recreated, as a sequel to our present relationship with God, by an act of God. He is the initiator, and he himself is our guarantee.

In conclusion, I have to agree with the compelling words penned by the German theologian, Helmut Thielicke:

> Faith in the so-called immortality of the soul is no faith at all. It is rather a highly questionable assumption, which can be made even by a complete heathen and worldling. One can make it without caring two pins for God. One can still make it, even if one considers the resurrection of the Lord a highly superfluous spectacle of pious fantasy. . . . There *is* no such thing as immortality; God *gives* immortality.[51]

Now, we can turn to the final question, How does God reveal his truths through the biblical data studied by theologians as compared with the personal data studied by psychologists?

Let us begin to answer by reviewing briefly what has been said about the nature of the Bible and the nature of the person. The *Bible* has a dual nature—part human and part divine—and has a servant-form. Also, the Bible's authority is experienced rather than simply accepted through proclamation. The *person* is created with the capacity to image God and to be indwelled by the Holy Spirit. In addition, the person's life after death is due to God's memory and re-creative act—it is not initiated by an immortal soul.

In considering the nature of the Bible, we emphasized the human element. In discussing the nature of the person, the relational element. Because of these emphases, the commonality of the way truth is known through the Bible and through the person is evident: truth is known through human/divine relationship. That answers the question, at least for the Christian (who is, after all, the only one who is likely to be interested in integrating psychology and Christianity). Truth is revealed through human/divine *biblical data* in the context of human interpretation guided by the Holy Spirit. Similarly, truth in the form of *personal data* is revealed to the human person in the context of human/divine encounter.

The foundation is now in place for the integration of psychology and Christianity, referred to as wholehearted integration and described as talking and walking with God. We have seen that, described in this way, integration is the same thing as fully knowing truth. The process begins with the Bible and the person. Because both are related to God by their inherent nature, the truths that God reveals through them are discernible in both cases by talking with him. There is no difference in the way God reveals his truths through biblical data and personal data. Likewise, the truths revealed through the one are no truer than the truths revealed through the other.

Talking with God through the Bible and the person has been viewed here as doing theology and psychology, respectively. However, we also saw that the communication process in both disciplines must and can be improved significantly. Should theological methods be examined before the facts that they produce are integrated? Yes. Would a transformed psychology enhance the quality of integration? Most definitely.

Wholehearted integration is talking *plus walking* with God. So the central idea has been that integration is not complete when it is intellectual only, although the two integration alternatives presented have contrasting emphases on that point. It was suggested, however, that one of the most effective integration methods of all would be a combination of the two approaches to balance Christian thinking with Christian living. It was also concluded that the thinking itself must be balanced; no one discipline should be the guardian discipline for protecting the truth.

Integration should be following Jesus Christ wholeheartedly in word and in deed. It should be a uniting in thought and application of what we really understand as true psychologically and theologically. By definition, this will not involve the entire discipline of psychology or the entire discipline of theology, nor will it even progress toward that. Wholehearted integration concerns only what God is showing us and expecting each of us to do in obedience to him. That is a privilege.

Notes

1. Holmes, A. F. *Contours of a world view.* Grand Rapids: Wm. B. Eerdmans, 1983, pp. 150–51.
2. Ibid., p. 148.
3. Maslow, A. H. *The Psychology of Science: A reconnaissance.* Chicago: Henry Regnery Gateway, 1966, chap. 6.
4. Koch, S. The nature and limits of psychological knowledge: Lessons of a century qua "science." *American Psychologist* 36 (1981): 257–69.
5. Ibid., pp. 259–60.
6. Ibid., p. 260.
7. Gould, S. J. *The mismeasure of man.* New York: W. W. Norton, 1981, pp. 21–22.
8. See J. M. Masson, *The assault on truth: Freud's suppression of the seduction theory.* New York: Farrar, Straus & Giroux, 1983; Kaye, K. Piaget's forgotten novel. *Psychology Today* 14(6) (1980): 102; Freeman, D. *Margaret Mead and Samoa: The making and unmaking of an anthropological myth.* Cambridge, Mass.: Harvard University, 1983.
9. See T. Mischel, Psychological explanations and their vicissitudes. In *Nebraska Symposium on Motivation 1975,* ed. J. K. Cole and W. J. Arnold. Lincoln: University of Nebraska, 1976, pp. 133–204.
10. Merleau-Ponty, M. *The primacy of perception and other essays on phenomenological psychology, the philosophy of art, history and politics,* trans. James M. Edie. Evanston, Ill.: Northwestern University, 1964.
11. Zajonc, R. B. Feeling and thinking: Preferences need no inferences. *American Psychologist* 35 (1980): 151–75; Zajonc, R. B. On the primacy of affect. *American Psychologist* 39 (1984): 117–23.
12. Einstein, A. Letter to Jacques Hadamard. In *The creative process: A symposium,* ed. B. Ghiselin. Berkeley and Los Angeles: University of California, 1952, pp. 32–33.

13. Tournier, P. *The meaning of persons,* trans. Edwin Hudson. New York: Harper & Row, 1957, p. 162.

14. Holmes, *Contours of a world view,* p. 142.

15. See A. Maslow, *The farther reaches of human nature*. New York: Viking, 1971, chap. 8.

16. Kierkegaard, S. *The last years: Journals 1853–1855,* trans. Ronald Gregor Smith. New York: Harper & Row, 1965, p. 133.

17. Thorson, W. R. The biblical insights of Michael Polanyi. *Journal of the American Scientific Affiliation* 33 (1981): 129–38, quotation on p. 136.

18. Ibid., p. 132.

19. Henry, C. F. H. *God, revelation and authority: Vol. 4, God who speaks and shows: Fifteen theses, part 3*. Waco: Word Books, 1979, p. 7.

20. Berkouwer, G. C. *Holy Scripture,* trans. Jack B. Rogers. Grand Rapids: Wm. B. Eerdmans, 1975, p. 24.

21. Ibid., see especially pp. 198–209.

22. Ibid., p. 19.

23. Ibid., p. 206.

24. Ramm, B. Misplaced battle lines. *The Reformed Journal* 26(6) (1976)37–38.

25. Berkouwer, *Holy Scripture,* p. 201.

26. Ibid., p. 33.

27. Ibid., pp. 33–34.

28. Ibid., pp. 34, 317.

29. Ibid., pp. 317–18.

30. Holmer, P. L. Contemporary evangelical faith: An assessment and critique. In *The evangelicals: What they believe, who they are, where they are changing,* ed. D. F. Wells and J. D. Woodbridge. New York: Abingdon, 1975, p. 73.

31. Ibid., p. 83.

32. Capon, R. F. *Hunting the divine fox: Images and mystery in Christian faith*. New York: Seabury, 1974, p. 133.

33. Lathbury, M. A. Break Thou the bread of life. In *Great hymns of the faith,* ed. J. W. Peterson. Grand Rapids: Zondervan, 1972, no. 176.

34. See J. V. Taylor, *Enough is enough: A biblical call for moderation in a consumer-oriented society*. Minneapolis: Augsburg, 1977, chap. 3.

35. Packer, J. I. *Knowing God*. Downers Grove, Ill: Inter-Varsity, 1973, p. 29.

36. Stott, J. R. W. *Men made new: An exposition of Romans 5–8*. Chicago: Inter-Varsity, 1966, p. 78.

37. Kushner, H. S. *When bad things happen to good people*. New York: Schocken Books, 1981, pp. 72–73.

38. See P. A. Bertocci, *Free will, responsibility; and grace*. New York: Abingdon, 1957, chap. 4.

39. Lewis, C. S. *Miracles: A preliminary study*. New York: Macmillan, 1947, pp. 206–7.

40. Buber, M. *I and thou,* trans. Walter Kaufmann. New York: Charles Scribner's Sons, 1970, p. 89.

41. Hatch, E. Breathe on me, Breath of God. In *Great hymns of the faith,* no. 164.

42. An important aspect of this definition is that it also safeguards against the subversion of human personality: "Paul makes explicitly clear that the presence of the Spirit or of Christ in a man does not operate purely dynamistically like a fluid welling up from subconscious depths to permeate and to comprise the content of all human life and

action. . . . To the classic statement that 'it is no longer I who live, but Christ who lives in me,' he immediately adds, 'the life I now live in the flesh I live by *faith* in the Son of God' (Gal. 2:20). . . . Christ (or the Spirit) is present, is our very life, only and always in the relational structure of *faith*." Come, A. B. *Human spirit and Holy Spirit*. Philadelphia: Westminster, 1959, pp. 115–16.

43. Lake, D. M. Mind. In *The Zondervan pictorial encyclopedia of the Bible: Vol. 4,* ed. M. C. Tenney. Grand Rapids: Zondervan, 1975, 1976, pp. 228–29, quotation on p. 229.

44. Holmes, A. F. Will. Ibid., *vol. 5,* p. 931.

45. Come, *Human spirit,* p. 37.

46. Holmes, *Contours of a world view,* pp. 110–11.

47. Bube, R. H., *The human quest: A new look at science and the Christian faith*. Waco: Word Books, 1971, chap. 7.

48. Myers, D. G., *The human puzzle: Psychological research and Christian belief*. San Francisco: Harper & Row, 1978, chap. 4.

49. *Ibid.*, p. 79.

50. MacKay, D. M. Brain research and human responsibility. In *Horizons of science: Christian scholars speak out,* ed. C. F. H. Henry. New York: Harper & Row, 1978, chap. 9.

51. Thielicke, H. *How the world began : Man in the first chapters of the Bible,* trans. John W. Doberstein. Philadelphia: Fortress, 1961, pp. 248–49. See also O. Cullmann, Immortality of the soul or resurrection of the dead? In *Immortality and resurrection,* ed. K. Stendahl. New York: Macmillan, 1965, pp. 9–53; Harris, M. Resurrection and immortality: Eight theses. *Themelios* 1 (1976): 50–55; Reichenbach, B. Life after death: Possible or impossible? *Christian Scholar's Review* 3 (1973): 232–44.

Bibliography

Adair, J. G. *The human subject: The social psychology of the psychological experiment*. Boston: Little, Brown and Company, 1973.

Anderson, G. H., & Stransky, T. F. (Eds.) *Mission trends no. 4: Liberation theologies in North America and Europe*. New York and Grand Rapids, MI: Paulist and Wm. B. Eerdmans, 1979.

Argyris, C. Some unintended consequences of rigorous research. *Psychological Bulletin,* 1968, *70,* 185–197.

Bakan, D. *On method: Toward a reconstruction of psychological investigation*. San Francisco: Jossey-Bass, 1967.

Bandura, A. The self system in reciprocal determinism. *American Psychologist,* 1978, *33,* 344–358.

Bassett, R. L., Basinger, D., & Livermore, P. Lying in the laboratory: Deception in human research from psychological, philosophical, and theological perspectives. *Journal of the American Scientific Affiliation,* 1982, *34,* 201–212.

Berkhof, H. *Christ and the powers,* trans. John H. Yoder. Scottdale, PA: Herald, 1977.

Berkouwer, G. C. *Holy Scripture,* trans. Jack B. Rogers. Grand Rapids, MI: Wm. B. Eerdmans, 1975.

Berkowitz, L. Simple views of aggression: An essay review. *American Scientist,* 1969, *57,* 372–383.

Bertocci, P. A. *Free will, responsibility, and grace*. New York: Abingdon, 1957.

Bolt, M., & Myers, D. G. *The human connection: How people change people*. Downers Grove, IL: Inter-Varsity, 1984.

Brown, R. M. Liberation theology: Paralyzing threat or creative challenge? In G. H. Anderson and T. F. Stransky (Eds.), *Mission trends no. 4: Liberation theologies in North America and Europe*. New York and Grand Rapids, MI: Paulist and Wm. B. Eerdmans, 1979, pp. 3–24.

Bube, R. H. *The human quest: A new look at science and the Christian faith*. Waco, TX: Word Books, 1971.

Buber, M. *I and thou,* trans. Walter Kaufmann. New York: Charles Scribner's Sons, 1970.

Bushnell, K. C. *God's word to women*. North Collins, NY: Ray B. Munson, 1923 (reprint).

Campbell, D. T. On the conflicts between biological and social evolution and between psychology and moral tradition. *American Psychologist,* 1975, *30,* 1103–1126.

Capon, R. F. *Hunting the divine fox: Images and mystery in Christian faith*. New York: Seabury, 1974.

Carter, J. D., & Narramore, B. *The integration of psychology and theology: An introduction:* Grand Rapids, MI: Zondervan, 1979.

Cherry, C. *The theology of Jonathan Edwards*. Garden City, NY: Doubleday, 1966.

Colaizzi, P. F. Psychological research as the phenomenologist views it. In R. S. Valle and M. King (Eds.), *Existential-phenomenological alternatives for psychology*. New York: Oxford University, 1978, ch. 3.

Collins, G. R. *The rebuilding of psychology: An integration of psychology and Christianity*. Wheaton, IL: Tyndale House, 1977.

———. *Psychology and theology: Prospects for integration*. Nashville: Abingdon, 1981.

Come, A. B. *Human spirit and Holy Spirit*. Philadelphia: Westminster, 1959.

Compaan, A. D. Biblical norms for career choice. *The CAPS Bulletin,* 1979, *5*(2), 12–17.

Cosgrove, M. P. *B.F. Skinner's behaviorism: An analysis*. Grand Rapids, MI: Zondervan, 1982.

Cox, H. Theology: What is it? Who does it? How is it done? *The Christian Century,* 1980, *97*(29), 874–879.

Crabb, L. J., Jr. *Effective biblical counseling*. Grand Rapids, MI: Zondervan, 1977.

———. Biblical authority and Christian psychology. *Journal of Psychology and Theology,* 1981, *9,* 305–311.

Cullmann, O. Immortality of the soul or resurrection of the dead? In K. Stendahl (Ed.), *Immortality and resurrection*. New York: Macmillan, 1965, pp. 9–53.

DeVries, M. J. Beyond integration: New directions. *The CAPS Bulletin,* 1981, 7(3), 1–5.

Donne, J. *Devotions upon emergent occasions.* Ann Arbor, MI: University of Michigan, 1960.

Dreyfus, H. L. *What computers can't do: A critique of artificial reason.* New York: Harper & Row, 1972.

Dueck, A., & Zerbe, G. Interpretations of Christ and Culture: The church, the world and the profession. Paper presented at the Christian Association for Psychological Studies Convention, Santa Barbara, June, 1976.

Ebersole, M. Conflict in clinical practice. Paper presented at the Eastern Area Mennonite Professionalism Conference, New York, February, 1979.

Einstein, A. Letter to Jacques Hadamard. In B. Ghiselin (Ed.), *The creative process: A symposium.* Berkeley and Los Angeles: University of California, 1952, pp. 32–33.

Ellens, J. H. Biblical themes in psychological theory and practice. *The CAPS Bulletin,* 1980, *6*(2), 2–6.

Ellul, J. *Hope in time of abandonment.* New York: Seabury, 1973.

Evans, C. S. *Preserving the person: A look at the human sciences.* Grand Rapids, MI: Baker Book House, 1982.

Everett, W. W., & Bachmeyer, T. J. *Disciplines in transformation: A guide to theology and the behavioral sciences.* Washington, D.C.: University Press of America, 1979.

Farnsworth, K. E. Christian psychotherapy and the culture of professionalism. *Journal of Psychology and Theology,* 1980, *8,* 115–121.

———. *Integrating psychology and theology: Elbows together but hearts apart.* Washington, D.C.: University Press of America, 1981.

———. The conduct of integration. *Journal of Psychology and Theology,* 1982, *10,* 308–319.

———. Furthering the kingdom in psychology. In A. Holmes (Ed.), *The making of a Christian mind: A Christian world view & the academic experience.* Downers Grove, IL: Inter-Varsity, 1985, ch. 4.

Farnsworth, K. E., Alexanian, J. M., & Iverson, J. D. Integration and the culture of rationalism: Reaction to responses to "the conduct of integration," part II. *Journal of Psychology and Theology,* 1983, *11,* 349–352.

Fleck, J. R., & Carter, J. D. (Eds.) *Psychology and Christianity: Integrative readings.* Nashville: Abingdon, 1981.

Foster, R. J. *Celebration of discipline: The path to spiritual growth.* New York: Harper & Row, 1978.

Frank, J. D. Nature and functions of belief systems: Humanism and transcendental religion. *American Psychologist,* 1977, *32,* 555–559.

Freeman, D. *Margaret Mead and Samoa: The making and unmaking of an anthropological myth*. Cambridge, MA: Harvard University, 1983.

Fromm, E. *Man for himself*. New York: Holt, Rinehart, & Winston, 1947.

Gelpi, D. L. *Experiencing God: A theology of human emergence*. New York: Paulist, 1978.

Gergen, K. J. Social psychology as history. *Journal of Personality and Social Psychology,* 1973, *26,* 309–320.

Giorgi, A. *Psychology as a human science: A phenomenologically based approach*. New York: Harper & Row, 1970.

———. The experience of the subject as a source of data in a psychological experiment. In A. Giorgi, W. F. Fischer, & R. Von Eckartsberg (Eds.), *Duquesne studies in phenomenological psychology: Volume I*. Pittsburgh: Duquesne University, 1971, ch. 4.

———. Phenomenology and the foundations of psychology. In J. K. Cole and W. J. Arnold (Eds.), *Nebraska symposium on motivation 1975*. Lincoln, NB: University of Nebraska, 1976, pp. 281–348.

Giorgi, A., Barton, A., & Maes, C. (Eds.) *Duquesne studies in phenomenological psychology: Volume IV*. Pittsburgh: Duquesne University, 1983.

Giorgi, A., Fischer, C. T., & Murray, E. L. (Eds.) *Duquesne studies in phenomenological psychology: Volume II*. Pittsburgh: Duquesne University, 1975.

Giorgi, A., Fischer, W. F., & Von Eckartsberg, R. (Eds.) *Duquesne studies in phenomenological psychology: Volume I*. Pittsburgh: Duquesne University, 1971.

Giorgi, A., Knowles, R., & Smith, D. L. (Eds.) *Duquesne studies in phenomenological psychology: Volume III*. Pittsburgh: Duquesne University, 1979.

Goleman, D. A conversation with Ulric Neisser. *Psychology Today,* 1983, *17*(5), 54-62.

Goodall, K. "This little girl won't interact with the other little girls, and she crawls around a lot": A conversation about behavior modification with Montrose M. Wolf. *Psychology Today,* 1973, 7(1), 64–72.

Gould, S. J. *The mismeasure of man*. New York: W. W. Norton, 1981.

Guy, J. D., Jr. Affirming diversity in the task of integration: A response to "biblical authority and Christian psychology." *Journal of Psychology and Theology,* 1982, *10,* 35–39.

Haas, J. W., Jr. Complementarity and Christian thought—An assessment: 2. Logical complementarity. *Journal of the American Scientific Affiliation,* 1983, *35,* 203–209.

Harlow, H. F., Harlow, M. K., & Suomi, S. J. From thought to therapy: Lessons from a primate laboratory. *American Scientist,* 1971, *59,* 538–549.

Harris, M. Resurrection and immortality: Eight theses. *Themelios,* 1976, *1,* 50–55.

Harris, T. G. Jung & old: An introduction. *Psychology Today,* 1971, *5*(7), 43.

Hatch, E. Breathe on me, Breath of God. In J. W. Peterson (Ed.), *Great hymns of the faith*. Grand Rapids, MI: Zondervan, 1972, no. 164.

Henry, C. F. H. (Ed.) *Horizons of science: Christian scholars speak out*. New York: Harper & Row, 1978.

———. *God, revelation and authority: Volume IV. God who speaks and shows: Fifteen theses, part three*. Waco, TX: Word Books, 1979.

Hirsch, E. D., Jr. *Validity in interpretation*. New Haven: Yale University, 1967.

Holmer, P. L. Contemporary evangelical faith: An assessment and critique. In D. F. Wells & J. D. Woodbridge (Eds.), *The evangelicals: What they believe, who they are, where they are changing*. New York: Abingdon, 1975, pp. 68–95.

Holmes, A. F. Will. In M.C. Tenney (Ed.), *The Zondervan pictorial encyclopedia of the Bible: Vol. 5*. Grand Rapids, MI: Zondervan, 1975, 1976, pp. 931–933.

———. *Contours of a world view.* Grand Rapids, MI: Wm. B. Eerdmans, 1983.

Hood, R. W., Jr. Religious orientation and the report of religious experience. *Journal for the Scientific Study of Religion,* 1970, *9,* 285–291.

Hutch, R. A. Jonathan Edwards' analysis of religious experience. *Journal of Psychology and Theology,* 1978, *6,* 123-131.

Jeeves, M. A. *Psychology and Christianity: The view both ways*. Downers Grove, IL: Inter-Varsity, 1976.

Johnson, C. B. *The psychology of biblical interpretation*. Grand Rapids, MI: Zondervan, 1983.

Kaplan, A. *The conduct of inquiry: Methodology for behavioral science*. San Francisco: Chandler, 1964.

Kaye, K. Piaget's forgotten novel. *Psychology Today,* 1980, *14*(6), 102.

Keen, E. *A primer in phenomenological psychology*. New York: Holt, Rinehart and Winston, 1975.

Kelsey, M. *Encounter with God: A theology of Christian experience*. Minneapolis: Bethany Fellowship, 1972.

Kierkegaard, S. *The last years: Journals 1853–1855,* trans. Ronald Gregor Smith. New York: Harper & Row, 1965.

Kilpatrick, W. K. *Psychological seduction: The failure of modern psychology*. New York: Thomas Nelson, 1983.

Koch, S. Language communities, search cells, and the psychological studies. In J. K. Cole & W. J. Arnold (Eds.), *Nebraska Symposium on Motivation 1975*. Lincoln, NB: University of Nebraska, 1976, pp. 477–559.

———. The nature and limits of psychological knowledge: Lessons of a century qua "science." *American Psychologist,* 1981, *36,* 257–269.

Kohlberg, L. Moral stages and moralization: The cognitive-developmental approach. In T. Lickona (Ed.), *Moral development and behavior: Theory, research, and social issues.* New York: Holt, Rinehart and Winston, 1976, ch. 2.

Koteskey, R. L. *Psychology from a Christian perspective.* Nashville: Abingdon, 1980.

Kraft, C. H. Can anthropological insight assist evangelical theology? *Christian Scholar's Review,* 1977, *7,* 165–202.

Kulik, J. A., Brown, D. R., Vestewig, R. E., & Wright, J. *Undergraduate education in psychology.* Washington, D. C.: American Psychological Association, 1973.

Kushner, H. S. *When bad things happen to good people.* New York: Schocken Books, 1981.

Lake, D. M. Mind. In M. C. Tenney (Ed.), *The Zondervan pictorial encyclopedia of the Bible: Vol. 4.* Grand Rapids, MI: Zondervan, 1975, 1976, pp. 228–229.

Lane, D. A. *The experience of God: An invitation to do theology.* New York: Paulist, 1981.

Larzelere, R. E. The task ahead: Six levels of integration of Christianity and psychology. *Journal of Psychology and Theology,* 1980, *8,* 3–11.

Lathbury, M. A. Break Thou the bread of life. In J. W. Peterson (Ed.), *Great hymns of the faith.* Grand Rapids, MI: Zondervan, 1972, no. 176.

Lewis, C. S. *The abolition of man.* New York: Macmillan, 1947.

———. *Miracles: A preliminary study.* New York: Macmillan, 1947.

Lewis, J., & Towers, B. *Naked ape or homo sapiens?* New York: New American Library, 1973.

Ludwig, T. E., Westphal, M., Klay, R. J., & Myers, D. G. *Inflation, poortalk, and the Gospel.* Valley Forge, PA: Judson, 1981.

Lyon, D. *Sociology and the human image.* Downers Grove, IL: Inter-Varsity, 1983.

MacKay, D. M. *The clockwork image: A Christian perspective on science.* Downers Grove, IL: Inter-Varsity, 1974.

———. Brain research and human responsibility. In C. F. H. Henry (Ed.), *Horizons of science: Christian scholars speak out.* New York: Harper & Row, 1978, ch. IX.

MacLeod, R. B. Psychological phenomenology: A propaedeutic to a scientific psychology. In J. R. Royce (Ed.) *Toward unification in psychology.* Toronto: University of Toronto, 1970, ch. 6.

———. *The persistent problems of psychology.* Pittsburgh: Duquesne University, 1975.

Malony, H. N. Religious experiencing: A phenomenological analysis of a unique behavioral event. *Journal of Psychology and Theology,* 1981, *9,* 326–334.

Maslow, A. H. *The psychology of science: A reconnaissance.* Chicago: Henry Regnery, 1966.

———. *The farther reaches of human nature.* New York: Viking, 1971.

Masson, J. M. *The assault on truth: Freud's suppression of the seduction theory.* New York: Farrar, Straus & Giroux, 1983.

May, R. *Psychology and the human dilemma.* Princeton, NJ: D. Van Nostrand, 1967.

McGuire, W. J. The yin and yang of progress in social psychology: Seven Koan. *Journal of Personality and Social Psychology,* 1973, *26,* 446–456.

Merleau-Ponty, M. *The primacy of perception and other essays on phenomenological psychology, the philosophy of art, history and politics,* trans. James M. Edie. Evanston, IL: Northwestern University, 1964.

———. What is phenomenology? trans. Colin Smith. In J. D. Bettis (Ed.), *Phenomenology of religion: Eight modern descriptions of the essence of religion.* New York: Harper & Row, 1969, pp. 13–30.

Meyer, D. *The positive thinkers: Religion as pop psychology from Mary Baker Eddy to Oral Roberts,* 2nd ed. New York: Pantheon Books, 1980.

Mickelsen, B., & Mickelsen, A. Does male dominance tarnish our translations? *Christianity Today,* 1979, *22*(23), 23–29.

Miller, A. G. (Ed.) *The social psychology of psychological research.* New York: The Free Press, 1972.

Mischel, T. Psychological explanations and their vicissitudes. In J. K. Cole & W. J. Arnold (Eds.), *Nebraska Symposium on Motivation 1975.* Lincoln, NB: University of Nebraska, 1976, pp. 133–204.

Misiak, H., & Sexton, V. S. *Phenomenological, existential, and humanistic psychologies: A historical survey.* New York: Grune & Stratton, 1973.

Mixter, R. L. (Ed.) *Evolution and Christian thought today,* 2nd ed. Grand Rapids, MI: Wm. B. Eerdmans, 1960.

Muson, H. Moral thinking: Can it be taught? *Psychology Today,* 1979, *12*(9), 48–68, 92.

Myers, D. G. *The human puzzle: Psychological research and Christian belief.* San Francisco: Harper & Row, 1978.

———. *The inflated self: Human illusions and the biblical call to hope.* New York: Seabury, 1981.

Needleman, C. Potter's progress: Self-understanding and the lessons of craft. *Psychology Today,* 1979, *13*(1), 78–86.

Niebuhr, H. R. *Christ and culture*. New York: Harper & Row, 1951.

Noll, M. Who sets the stage for understanding Scripture? *Christianity Today*, 1980, *24*(10), 14–18.

Oden, T. C. *The intensive group experience: The new pietism*. Philadelphia: Westminster, 1972.

Orlebeke, C. J. Donald MacKay's philosophy of science. *Christian Scholar's Review*, 1977, *7*, 51–63.

Orne, M. T. Hypnosis, motivation, and the ecological validity of the psychological experiment. In W. J. Arnold and M. M. Page (Eds.), *Nebraska symposium on motivation 1970*. Lincoln, NB: University of Nebraska, 1971, pp. 187–265.

Otto, R. *The idea of the holy: An inquiry into the non-rational factor in the idea of the divine and its relation to the rational*, trans. John W. Harvey, 2nd ed. New York: Oxford University, 1950.

Packer, J. I. *Knowing God*. Downers Grove, IL: Inter-Varsity, 1973.

Padilla, C. R. Liberation theology (II): An evaluation. *The Reformed Journal*, 1983, *33*(7), 14–18.

Peale N. V. *You can win*. Nashville: Abingdon, 1938.

Ramm, B. Misplaced battle lines. *The Reformed Journal*, 1976, *26*(6), 37–38.

Reese, B. Within or outside the system: An Anabaptist perspective. Paper presented at the Eastern Area Mennonite Professionalism Conference, New York, February, 1979.

Reichenbach, B. Life after death: Possible or impossible? *Christian Scholar's Review*, 1973, *3*, 232–244.

Robinson, J. P., & Shaver, P. R. (Eds.) *Measures of social psychological attitudes*. Ann Arbor, MI: Institute for Social Research, 1973.

Rokeach, M. *The open and closed mind*. New York: Basic Books, 1960.

Rosenthal, R. *Experimenter effects in behavioral research*. New York: Appleton-Century-Crofts, 1966.

Royce, J. R. (Ed.) *Psychology and the symbol: An interdisciplinary symposium*. New York: Random House, 1965.

Rubin, Z. Taking deception for granted. *Psychology Today*, 1983, *17*(3), 74–75.

Sanford, N. *Issues in personality theory*. San Francisco: Jossey-Bass, 1970.

Sargant, W. *Battle for the mind: A physiology of conversion and brain-washing*. London: William Heinemann, 1957.

Shostrom, E. L., & Montgomery, D. *Healing love: How God works within the personality*. Nashville: Abingdon, 1978.

Snygg, D., & Combs, A. W. *Individual behavior: A new frame of reference for psychology*. New York: Harper & Row, 1949.

Solzhenitsyn, A. I. *A world split apart: Commencement address delivered at Harvard University, June 8, 1978,* trans. Irina Ilovayskaya Alberti. New York: Harper & Row, 1978.

Spiegelberg, H. *The phenomenological movement: A historical introduction,* 2nd ed. The Hague, Netherlands: Martinus Nijhoff, 1969.

———. *Phenomenology in psychology and psychiatry: A historical introduction.* Evanston, IL: Northwestern University, 1972.

Stevick, E. L. An empirical investigation of the experience of anger. In A. Giorgi, W. F. Fischer, and R. Von Eckartsberg (Eds.), *Duquesne studies in phenomenological psychology: Volume I.* Pittsburgh: Duquesne University, 1971, ch. 10.

Stones, C. R. Research: Toward a phenomenological praxis. In D. Kruger, *An introduction to phenomenological psychology*. Pittsburgh: Duquesne University, 1981, ch. 4.

Stott, J. R. W. *Men made new: An exposition of Romans 5–8.* Chicago: Inter-Varsity, 1966.

Taylor, J. V. *Enough is enough: A biblical call for moderation in a consumer-oriented society*. Minneapolis: Augsburg, 1977.

Thielicke, H. *How the world began: Man in the first chapters of the Bible,* trans. John W. Doberstein. Philadelphia: Fortress, 1961.

Thorson, W. R. The spiritiual dimensions of science. In C.F.H. Henry (Ed.), *Horizons of science: Christian scholars speak out*. New York: Harper & Row, 1978, ch. XI.

———. The biblical insights of Michael Polanyi. *Journal of the American Scientific Affiliation,* 1981, *33,* 129–138.

Tournier, P. *The meaning of persons,* trans. Edwin Hudson. New York: Harper & Row, 1957.

Valle, R. S., & von Eckartsberg, R. (Eds.) *The metaphors of consciousness*. New York: Plenum, 1981.

van Kaam, A. *Existential foundations of psychology*. Pittsburgh: Duquesne University, 1966.

Van Leeuwen, M. S. *The sorcerer's apprentice: A Christian look at the changing face of psychology.* Downers Grove, IL: Inter-Varsity, 1982.

Wallach, M. A., & Wallach, L. *Psychology's sanction for selfishness: The error of egoism in theory and therapy*. San Francisco: W. H. Freeman, 1983.

Wann, T. W. (Ed.) *Behaviorism and phenomenology: Contrasting bases for modern psychology*. Chicago: University of Chicago, 1964.

Weber, S. J., & Cook, T. D. Subject effects in laboratory research: An examination of subject roles, demand characteristics, and valid inference. *Psychological Bulletin,* 1972, *77,* 273–295.

Wells, D. F., & Woodbridge, J. D. (Eds.) *The evangelicals: What they believe, who they are, where they are changing,* rev. ed. Grand Rapids, MI: Baker Book House, 1977.

Willems, E. P., & Rausch, H. L. (Eds.) *Naturalistic viewpoints in psychological research.* New York: Holt, Rinehart and Winston, 1969.

Wolterstorff, N. *Reason within the bounds of religion.* Grand Rapids, MI: Wm. B. Eerdmans, 1976.

———. The Bible and women: Another look at the "conservative" position. *The Reformed Journal,* 1979, *29*(6), 23–26.

———. *Educating for responsible action.* Grand Rapids, MI: Wm. B. Eerdmans, 1980.

Yoder, J. H. "Christ and culture": A critique of H. Richard Niebuhr. Unpublished paper, 1976.

Zajonc, R. B. Feeling and thinking: Preferences need no inferences. *American Psychologist,* 1980, *35,* 151–175.

———. On the primacy of affect. *American Psychologist,* 1984, *39,* 117–123.

Index